ABBATT
TOYS

ABBATT TOYS

MODERN TOYS FOR MODERN CHILDREN

ALAN POWERS

———

DESIGN FOR TODAY
2021

First published in 2020 by Design For Today
Revised edition 2021
88 Emmanuel Road, London, SW 12 0HR
www.designfortoday.co.uk

Text © Alan Powers 2021

ISBN: 978-1-912066-74-2

Set in Futura PT and Adobe Garamond Pro

Printed at Graphius, Ghent, Belgium

Designed by Laurence Beck & Joe Pearson

Cover: London bus from *Street* picture tray
designed by Madeleine Robinson, 1935
Endpaper: Abbatt logo designed by Ernö Goldfinger,
1933, from *Airplane Snakes & Ladders*, 1938
Title page and contents page: Horse and Farmhouse from *Farmyard*
picture tray designed by Freda Skinner, 1933

★ ★ ★ ★
DESIGN FOR TODAY
ephemera, objects of curiosity, books to read and touch

CONTENTS

Paul and Marjorie Abbatt showroom, 94 Wimpole Street, London W1, designed by Ernö Goldfinger

INTRODUCTION

The names 'Paul and Marjorie Abbatt' or 'Abbatt Toys', combined with their logo of a boy and girl in silhouette, holding hands, will be lodged in the deep memory of many living people. From 1932 to 1973, this was the name of a London-based company manufacturing and selling children's toys which was, for most of that time, the chief exponent of the idea of modern toys in Britain.

A modern toy not only looks modern, in terms of the simplicity and abstractness of the twentieth century design style, but it works in a modern way too, calibrated to an observed stage of development, lacking any obvious gender differentiation but intended to offer more than the usual amount of 'affordance' of the average commercial equivalent – or in plain words, the simpler it is, the more things you can do with it.

The inspiration that led two people into a lifetime's work came, as many modern things came to Britain in the 1930s, from continental Europe, supported by experiments in child rearing and teaching closer to home. Paul and Marjorie Abbatt Ltd. was a business, but it was also a research project and a mission. It was unashamedly 'progressive', in line with other activism by the educated and privileged aimed at spreading more 'enlightened' practices as widely as possible, including among the middle and upper classes whose concept of child-rearing was often distressingly primitive and damaging.

Paul and Marjorie were, like other progressives, escapees from their own childhood environments. Paul was afflicted more by bleak surroundings than by repressive ideas, despite the family business, William Abbatt & Co.

manufacturing punishment canes known as 'Abbatt's Persuaders' as a sideline to their main business making baskets and skips from cane.[1] Paul was born on 19 July, 1899 at Bromley Cross, near Bolton, Lancashire, to a Quaker family in one of the centres of the cotton spinning industry. Educated at long-established Quaker schools in Yorkshire, he studied Natural Sciences at Cambridge before becoming a teacher himself at Sidcot in Somerset, a Quaker school with a noted scientific tradition. Here he came into contact with the Order of Woodcraft Chivalry, founded in 1916 as one of several pacifist alternatives to the Boy Scouts, the ethos of which pervaded the school. Educational in the widest sense and based on 'learning by doing', Woodcraft became the centre of Paul's interest and activities, and it was at one of the Order's annual 'Folkmoots', with a gathering of members in home-made tents, that he met Marjorie in 1926.

Norah Marjorie Cobb was also born in 1899 and grew up in Surrey. The Cobb family owned a private bank based in East Kent which was amalgamated with Lloyds in 1891 after losses incurred by her grandfather. Her father was a fur trader and both parents were socially conventional. Marjorie became a pupil at Roedean School near Brighton, known for its progressive approach, proceeding in 1918 to Somerville College, Oxford. Here she

flourished among a determined body of women students. As a profile in *The Times Educational Supplement* in 1973 explained, 'Her work began in reaction to family pressure which would have forced her into a conventional pattern. She rebelled, chose her friends among intellectuals.'[2] By 1926, when she met Paul at the Godshill Folkmoot, Marjorie had enrolled at University College, London, to study for an MD in psychoanalysis and speech therapy, intending to become a practitioner.

Paul became a teacher at the forest school at Godshill when it was opened by Ernest Westlake in 1929. Some of his letters to Marjorie in 1928 survive, in which they address each other as Rat and Mole (after *The Wind in the Willows*). Recalling later 'I always felt that I had been subject to so much interruption', Marjorie seems to have experienced a moment of revelation, 'to find myself in a little teeny tent in the woods which smelt so marvellously – all the pine trees, you know – and to hear the birds singing in the morning. I felt quite ecstatic about it … and there I met my husband.'[3]

All this was different to her parents' intentions for her. Falling in love with Paul at first meeting worried them more and they were married only in December 1930, having travelled together the previous summer on a folk-

Alison   Granny   Marjorie

Mrs Cobb with her daughters Alison (left) Marjorie (right)

dancing tour in Germany. Thinking at first that they would establish their own school, Paul and Marjorie's ideas changed during their extended honeymoon during 1931, determining them instead to make their name through selling toys as 'tools for development' first.[4]

The honeymoon itinerary included Austria, the then-Yugoslavia and Russia, furnished with a letter of introduction to the Austrian Minister of Education from his English counterpart, Sir Charles Trevelyan. As Paul recalled in 1957, 'We visited various schools there which were lively and advanced in method. As I had been a schoolmaster, it was of great interest to me to sit at the back of the classes and notice the way in which the children were drawn in to play an active part in whatever subject or problem was under discussion.' In the nursery schools they were 'intrigued to find the little children quietly and interestedly engaged in occupations.'[5]

Their most important discoveries took place during their first four months in Vienna. Here they met Helen Low-Beer, who in turn introduced them to Milan Morgenstern (1895-1954), a specialist in the training of disabled children, whose methods, then working in Berlin and developing a method that he called *Heilpädagogie*, a combination of therapy and child training.

Two other Bauhaus students of the same generation, Franz Singer (1896-1954) and Friedl Dicker (1898-1944), were working together in Vienna and designed the interiors for the Montessori kindergarten at the Goethehof, Schüttaustrasse in 1931. Singer later settled in London as an émigré, but prior to his permanent relocation in 1938, and designed the showroom part of the Abbatts' building in Midford Place, Tottenham Court Road, when it opened in 1934, with Ernö Goldfinger having responsibility for the remainder.

Jude Welton quotes Marjorie's memories from 1980, 'the Sandleiten nursery [recently rehoused as part of a Modernist housing complex], where each child had a drawer full of equipment and toys that were private to the individual and the *Haus der Kinder* run by Lili Rowbiczek [also in a new building by Franz Schuster]. This school was furnished, not only with Montessori materials, but scaled-down domestic equipment and child-sized tables and chairs built by a local carpenter.'[6] She also recalled a set of Bauhaus drinking mugs, but these seem to be the only direct references to the famous school apart from their brief engagement with Ludwig Hirschfeld-Mack in 1938-9. In the limited visual reporting of Bauhaus productions in British journals and books, no toys were featured, and there is no direct evidence that they knew

Haus der Kinder, Vienna
designed by Franz Schuster

about the work of Alma Siedhof-Büscher, the main contributor from the Bauhaus to the development of toys and children's furniture. It might otherwise be tempting to claim her as a precursor for the Abbatts' work.

Maria Montessori (1870-1952) and her 'Method', based on freedom and tactile learning, was known in Britain through a translation from the original Italian in 1912. She stressed the importance of child-centred learning, with furniture and equipment of appropriate size and scale. There were longer historical roots for the pedagogy of Friedrich Froebel with the Froebel Trust in 1874 active in publishing, and the Froebel College for teacher training founded in 1892, both still operating. The similar theories of the American, John Dewey (1859-1952), emphasising 'learning by doing', were promoted by Dr Findlay at the University of Manchester in a book of 1906.

Margaret McMillan (1860-1931) and her sister Rachel (1859-1917), social idealists and activists, were campaigners for the welfare and nurture of poorer children from the beginning of the century and moved from provision of independent child welfare centres in London to found the Open-Air Nursery School and Training Centre in Deptford, later renamed in memory of Rachel.[7] Two items in an early Abbatt catalogue of 1934 are described as 'the Margaret McMillan toys', a sorting board (wooden shapes to be threaded onto spindles) and a 'Box of Shapes', consisting of coloured triangles).

They also met Franz Cizek (1865-1946), already famous in England owing to the promotion of his work with child art by the teacher and humanitarian worker, Francesca Wilson (1888-1981), who became an advocate after meeting him in a bleak and impoverished post-1918 Vienna, becoming 'entranced by his methods and determined to disseminate his pedagogical practices', which she did by exhibitions and publications.[8] The reality of Cizek's classes, in which children were encouraged to work to suggestion but without many constraints, chimed with Paul's experience as a teacher and also with the new book, *Intellectual Growth in Young Children*, 1930, by the teacher and psychoanalyst, Susan Isaacs (1885-1948), one of several publications in which she established a commanding position in the field after several years' experience at the Malting House (1924-27), a progressive school in Cambridge.[9]

The end of the book deals specifically with the toys and equipment used at the Malting House, most of which seem to have been custom-made since no trade products existed. Among other features of the school, the

Maria Montessori visiting a Montessori school in Acton, West London, 1946

Susan Isaacs with children at the Malting House School, Cambridge, c.1927

availability of real tools and craft materials encouraged tactile experiment, trusting to children's own sense of safety. Learning was not abstract, but translated into visual form and held in the hand. As Jude Welton summarises, 'play was the children's work'.[10] Perhaps the most representative product was the wooden garden climbing frame or 'jungle gym', which became a stock Abbatt product for the lifespan of the company.

At the thirty-year point of their business, an unsigned profile in the *Observer* irreverently captured their interaction as 'a partnership as indissoluble, and as redolent of a period, as the union of the Lunts' [Alfred Lunt and Lynne Fontanne, American actors]. Paul and Marjorie were described respectively as 'a dapper man of considerable charm … [and] an elegant woman with the russet colouring of some famous English beauties. Even the interplay of the two voices has an unconscious hint of stage dialogue – the clipped accents and well-chosen phrases of the mellowing don, the deep-throated Roedean rejoinders. The subject is nearly always play.'[11] They kept their watches permanently set to British Summer Time, 'to be sure of starting work at 8 a.m.'

During their earlier lives and their travels, the Abbatts seem to have laid the foundations for their careers, without knowing what these would be. They did not invent many things from scratch, but they brought existing ideas and play materials from different places together and then created a vehicle for promoting both the things and the ideas in combination, not only to professionals in the field, but also to the general public.

While still holding the idea in their minds of starting a school, they 'wanted to start with enough money for a large staff.' With the world in economic turmoil, the first years of the 1930s were not the most propitious time for finding backers, so that the welcome given to their first venture, an exhibition of toys, put them on a different path.

29 Tavistock Square, WC1, home of Paul and Marjorie Abbatt. 1932-39

ABBATTS IN BLOOMSBURY

'Paul and Marjorie Abbatt, whoever they may be, have collaborated to more purpose than most companions in intellectual production, for they have created a new series of toys that seem destined for a long and successful course in the juvenile region that so narrowly divides recreation from instruction. Yet there is nothing didactic or super-educational about the Abbatt toys – simply an adaptation of the Montessori principle of allowing intelligent youngsters to work out their educational salvation for themselves.'[12]

Thirty years later, they described their objectives as '*a departure from the usual*' in the world of toys, where the aim had often been to attract the adult by the comic, the pretty or the ingenious. So often the child found the container or wrapping, even the string, a more acceptable plaything than the expensive toy enclosed. The new project brought into focus the child-user – his stage of development, the aims of his play.'[13]

'Whoever they may be' was something the English world was already beginning to discover when this account was printed of a display of their products at Waring and Gillow's showrooms in Oxford Street in December 1934. Three years earlier, after an exciting trip to Russia and a return visit to Vienna, where they collected samples of toys, the couple returned to London. They followed up with visits to the Leipzig Toy Fair in the spring following, touring factories in Germany and also calling at the Maison des Petits in Geneva, founded in 1913 as a research centre attached to the university and originally named after Jean-Jacques Rousseau. Jean Piaget (1895-1980), who became famous for his work on child development, did some early studies of children here.

The Abbatts held an exhibition of the toys they had collected in the front room of their flat at 29 Tavistock Square in Bloomsbury for six weeks in June and July, 1932, while they camped out in the back room. In Paul's account, 'The items as I remember them were mainly tools for housekeeping, all the appropriate size for children's use. The brooms and brushes were all strong and useable, and were not made childish by decorations of the mickey mouse kind. The wringer, the clothes horse and the ironing-board were likewise not the real articles for grown-ups, nor were they toys for pretend-play only; they were miniatures, but strong and workmanlike.' These and other things, he commented with hindsight, had become commonplace, 'but then it conveyed a new attitude to childhood, and one which we worked to show to our friends in England.' He named some of the sources, such as large bricks from the Pestalozzi-Froebel House in Berlin, nests of boxes from Leipzig and 'fitting toys' from an American friend in London.[14]

This gave them confidence to start 'to manufacture, to market, in fact to go into business. From our first business systems of noting transactions on the backs of envelopes and keeping the takings in a different pocket from our personal money, we gradually learnt the mysteries of cash books, ledgers and bank accounts.' The business was registered as a limited company on 23 September 1932, with a nominal capital in £100 shares. An interview with Marjorie in 1973 explained that 'the terms of the lease [in Tavistock Square] prohibited retail sales, so they built up a mailing-list.' There must have been a considerable outlay as they rented four floors of Nos. 7-8 Midford Place, off Tottenham Court Road as a factory, stockroom and offices, retaining the site until the outbreak of the Second World War. Until the shop and showroom in Wimpole Street opened in 1936, it remained a mail-order business, which especially suited sales to schools, for which catalogues played a significant role, designed with care and projecting a friendly modernist image. The first was illustrated by the sculptor John Skeaping, known for his depiction of animals and the first husband of Barbara Hepworth.[15]

Both the flat and the Midford Place building were fitted out by the architect Ernö Goldfinger (1902-1988), on whose expanding reputational coat-tails the name of Abbatt has been kept alive in recent decades. How the Abbatts met the Hungarian Goldfinger and his English wife, Ursula Blackwell, remains unknown.[16] They clearly became close friends at the outset, and Paul was asked to become godfather to their son John Peter, born in September 1933, when the couple were still living in

Farmyard picture tray, designed by Freda Skinner, 1933, (13 x 18 inches)

'Nursery' section *Exhibition of British Industrial Art in Relation to the Home,* 1933. Designer Oliver Hill

Paris. In 1935, they moved permanently to London where Goldfinger was involved in many design projects that failed to come to fruition, so that his work for Abbatts was a significant part of his practice in these early years, for which he received a retainer of ten guineas a month plus royalties on sales of his designs, until financial stringency in 1938 brought it to an end. His office in Bedford Square was only five minutes' walk from Tavistock Square or Midford Place. His involvement with the Abbatts and their company is described in greater detail in the following chapters.

The workforce at Midford Place was chiefly involved in the production of wooden items for sale, other trades being contracted out. The Goldfinger archive reveals that they also took on outside joinery work on commission, and in 1935, at the invitation of fellow émigré architect Berthold Lubetkin, who proposed that they might be jointly engaged in fitting out the newly-completed flats in his first Highpoint block in Highgate, where the Goldfingers themselves lived before completing their own house in Hampstead.[17]

Exhibitions

The Abbatts were quick to show their work in a series of design exhibitions in London that signalled the beginning of a coherent Modernist look in Britain, derived from European examples but in most cases modified to suit English tastes. In 1932, the reform-minded government, faced with a severe recession, returned to the Victorian idea that by improving British industrial design, new export markets could be opened to trade. In fact, tariff barriers were rising at this time, but one effect was to deter the import of foreign goods and encourage the manufacture of equivalent products at home. Many over-optimistic ventures were launched for furniture, light fittings and other household goods, but the Abbatts had an expanding market with an increased awareness, also generated by the Slump, that education needed reform along with other aspects of life, as the Hadow Report foreshadowed.

Cover of *Design For To-day*, with article by Paul Abbatt,
December 1933

Upper right : *Factory* building blocks by Ladislav Sutnar.
Lower right : Selection of toys illustrated in Paul Abbatt's article,
showing *Colour Tower*, *Posting Box*, *Nest of Boxes*, *Six Peg Block*,
Peg Train, *First Train* and *Peg and Block Trolley*

One of their new London contacts was a child psychologist, Margaret Lowenfeld (1890-1973), whose work with children involved sand play and the use of toy animals in what she called 'The World Technique'. Lowenfeld may have been their link to the architect Oliver Hill (1887-1968) who was the overall designer and selector for the long-windedly named *Exhibition of British Industrial Art in Relation to the Home*, held in Lower Regent Street in July 1933. This proved to be a runaway success with 1,500 visitors a day. Although the organisation is often attributed to the Design and Industries Association, their earlier plans for an exhibition never came to fruition, and Christopher Hussey of *Country Life* magazine, with Oliver Hill as his henchman, took the initiative.

The Nursery section was selected by the Abbatts and designed by Hill. A single known photograph of the installation can be correlated to the items listed in the catalogue, including Pomona Toys of Holland Street, Kensington – mainly updated versions of Victorian 'Dutch Dolls' – and other painted wooden toys by Mary Horder.[18] Driven by educational theory, the Abbatt toys tended to be more austere than the other items. In this time of retreating internationalism and higher import tariffs, the *Edinburgh Evening News* noted that, while many wooden toys had recently been imported from the USA, Sweden and Russia, these were now challenged by 'solid Empire woods [which] although light in weight, are far more durable than the hollow, more flimsily-assembled foreign article.'[19]

As part of the resurgence of interest in design, again backed by *Country Life*, the DIA launched its glossiest magazine to date, *Design for To-day*, in the spring of 1933. Paul Abbatt contributed to the December issue (often the only moment in the year when toys got an airing), and the cover showed a grouping of toys, including a number of fabric dolls with faces painted onto moulded buckram by Norah Wellings (1893-1975). In production since 1926, these were markedly different to the standard baby dolls, and often featured dolls of non-white character. Paul Abbatt's text, 'The Child's World: Psychology in Toys and Games', rehearses the issues about appropriate toys that hardly varied through the lifetime of the business, and the photographs are useful for showing how much of the range of their own products had taken shape by this time, combined with items from other suppliers.[20] Several of the photographs were by 'Lisa' (Lisa Sheridan, 1894-1966), a photographer of Russian origin, noted for her informal portraits of the royal family from 1936 onwards.[21] Others were taken by Vogue Studios.

The article opened with two pictures of toys designed by the Czech graphic designer, Ladislav Sutnar (1897-1976), who later transformed the New York telephone directory but started his career in the 1920s as a designer of toys and puppets. Strictly architectural but brightly coloured, these included his *Build the Town* set of blocks, with tall factory chimneys, and a kitchen set (p.22). The photos with black backgrounds may have come direct from the designer.

Whereas Oliver Hill had contributed some rather heavy-looking furniture in 1933, a successor exhibition, *Contemporary Industrial Design* held in 1934, included another Abbatt nursery, this time credited to Ernö and Ursula jointly, with newly-designed chairs and fitted cupboard units, two of which were made as 'tiny trollies', plus stacking tables, chairs and rest-beds 'designed for correct sitting and lying postures.'[22] 'In the decoration of the present nursery', ran the descriptive text, almost certainly by Paul, 'the furniture and the toys are designed to be of real assistance to the child. They suit his needs – the first consideration – and aim at a high standard of beauty in proportion, line, material and colour.'[23]

A typed description in the Goldfinger archive, dated 31 May 1934, possibly referring to the same project, emphasises compactness safety and hygiene but also bright colours and pin-up surfaces. Even so, it is hard to avoid correlating this vision with the kind of bleak progressive nursery caricatured by Osbert Lancaster and contrasted with a cosy, cluttered Victorian equivalent overseen by a comfortable nanny. The text concludes 'All forms of pictorial decoration are scrupulously avoided. The child's taste is left to develop naturally. The nursery is a room in which he may rest & play with toys, books & pictures that change to meet the needs of rapidly growing intelligence. But as he unquestioningly accepts his own surroundings as being right, it is of paramount importance that his own room should be beautiful in form, proportion and colour.'[24] Writing in 1935, Marjorie Abbat described a nursery by the Goldfingers with translucent curtains of blue oilsilk, one blue wall, one white and a third the colour of red earth, and a blue linoleum tabletop and brightly coloured cupboard doors.

It should be emphasised that at all periods, the stock in the Abbatt catalogue and shop was only partly made up of their own proprietary products. The printed records are, however, unhelpful so far as distinguishing between items is concerned, since no distinction is made, at least in the early years. The presence of other products comes through in a commentary by H. Pearl Adams of the *Observer* in December 1934, 'Paul and Marjorie Abbatt continue to

LADY LITTLEHAMPTON VISITING THE NURSERY, *CIRCA* 1900

Osbert Lancaster,
Lady Littlehampton visitng the nursery, 1950

LADY LITTLEHAMPTON VISITING THE NURSERY, *CIRCA* 1950

enlarge the number of their very attractive playthings. Their wooden animals draw the happy mean between realism and that particular kind of "quaintness" which so many children happily detest. The shifting and matching wooden toys continue their good work of convincing the child that he is having a lovely game, while meanwhile teaching him a great deal about form and colour. The jigsaws for small children are equally useful and amusing, and so are the picture-trays from which all the objects can be lifted out by little knobs and used as models for drawing.'[25]

The same writer followed up a few months later, praising 'The Modern Tendency' in toys as a welcome change from the era that has been called that of 'the precious child', as she caricatured it, 'fond parents, with brows so high that birds nested in their hair, would have nothing less than Raphael Madonnas and Della Robbia Bambini on the walls of their nurseries; and talk Ruskinese to their children.' While she disparaged 'adult seekings for the deliberately childish', and had a swipe at 'grave spectacled men wearing rubber shoes and white overalls, in remote laboratories, who are bending the most abstruse branches of chemistry to the noble end of making a toy both bright and suckable', she was pleased with the general direction and mentioned the Abbatt 'fit-in' toys (the picture trays)

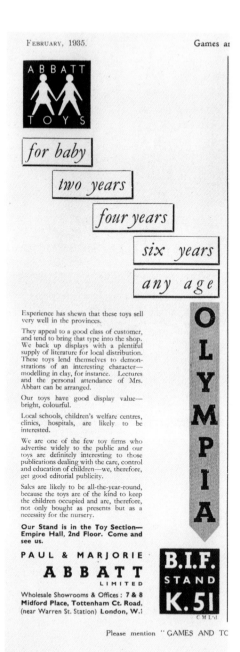

Advertisements for Abbatt, from *Games and Toys*. 1935

satisfying

entertaining

educational

Enterprising retailers who stock and display ABBATT TOYS attract customers with money to spend. Paul and Marjorie Abbatt sell only toys of tested popularity with children, and appealing to modern parents making a study of their children's welfare and development, both mental and physical.

PAUL & MARJORIE

ABBATT

LIMITED

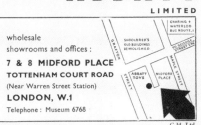

wholesale
showrooms and offices :

7 & 8 MIDFORD PLACE
TOTTENHAM COURT ROAD
(Near Warren Street Station)
LONDON, W.1
Telephone : Museum 6768

TOYS " when writing to advertisers.

that 'simplify the nursery's notion of what a train is, or a road-coach, and allow room for the budding imagination to develop itself by supplying details.'[26] From Dartington School in Devon, they adopted the double-sided easel on which two children could work together, a simple and much copied idea.

Jude Welton notes, probably repeating Marjorie's memories, that 'they tended not to place advertisements in *The Toy Trader* … preferring to stress the educational and design appeal of their toys, rather than the commercial.'[27] Edward Newmark, who later worked with the Abbatts, described the attitude of the majority of the trade in these terms, 'all this research is most interesting and no doubt valuable – but let us get on with the comparatively simple business of making and selling toys.'[28]

Despite this, another magazine, *Games & Toys*, aimed at retailers on behalf of manufacturers, 'discovered' Abbatt in 1935, writing enthusiastically about their catalogues, the jigsaws and outdoor toys, illustrating the Funboat with a determined small girl apparently setting the pace with a rather surprised-looking boy. The article was a trailer for the stand they took at the British Industries Fair (BIF) at Olympia in March, where there was a major section for toys. Although their stand was one of the smallest, and the magazine praised its attractiveness and particularly the kindergarten toys, evidently a sector not well served by other brands, concluding 'they are beautifully finished and very nicely made.'[29] The catalogues must have been quite widely distributed, being offered free by post to any readers of *Nursery World* magazine in December 1935.[30]

Advertising their presence at the BIF, they paraded a fairly shameless snobbery to the retailers they hoped to attract, writing 'Experience has shewn that these toys sell very well in the provinces. They appeal to a good class of customer, and tend to bring that type into the shop. … Our toys lend themselves to demonstrations of an interesting character – modelling in clay, for instance. Lectures and the personal attendance of Mrs. Abbatt can be arranged.'[31]

After noting the good display value of their bright colours, they emphasised how institutions involved in child care would be attracted, and interest would be supported by good editorial publicity in relevant publications. Furthermore, retailers might expect to sell Abbatt toys more regularly year-round rather than just at Christmas, 'because the toys are of the kind to keep the children occupied and are, therefore, not only bought as presents but as a necessity for the nursery.'[32]

Before opening their own shop in 1936, the Abbatts relied either on mail order or supplying other retailers. An advertisement of 1934 lists six outlets in London, including Hamley's, Harrods, Heal & Son., Selfridge's and Waring & Gillow. Thirty-one other towns and cities are listed, encompassing some shops whose reputation for good design has been transmitted from the time, such as P. E. Gane of Bristol, soon to become patrons of Marcel Breuer, Kendal Milne of Manchester where Walter Gropius created a model flat exhibition, and Rowntree's of Scarborough.

They were not alone in the kind of products they made. In 1932, Hilary 'Harry' Fisher Page (1904-1957) founded Kiddicraft, and produced a hammer peg and sorting box almost identical to the Abbatt equivalents. These were advertised with the slogan 'Child psychologists will tell you that every baby should be given this first toy'. He also made a number of stained colour wooden toys on wheels that could be assembled by the child.[33]

After 1936, Page moved increasingly to the production of plastic items, party owing to his concern about the hygiene of wooden toys. Another rival in the field was Betty Bashall, who acted as both designer and manufacturer for her company based at Thames Ditton,

Hammer Pegs,
made by Kiddicraft, c 1935,

which turned during the war years to making Mosquito aircraft. Her designs for sit-on horses and cars were brightly painted, but she also made items that were Abbatt-like in their earnest practicality, such as a small-scale carpentry bench, a portable sandpit 'painted jade and yellow with a striped orange canopy' and a tray with flowerpots and a small watering can.[34]

Nursery Schools and the Hadow Report

In respect of a general enthusiasm for nursery education, the Abbatts' timing in starting their business was good. In 1933 the Hadow Report on nursery education up to the age of 7+, set up in 1931 during the second Labour administration of Ramsay MacDonald, a vice-president of the Association, supported nursery schools 'as a desirable adjunct to the national system of education', recommending their provision with garden playgrounds in housing schemes.[35] For a government document, it seems, especially in the light of recent policy, remarkably enlightened for its time, recognising not only that Froebel and Montessori (who appeared in person to give evidence, together with Susan Isaacs), were important, but that their ideas must be understood and implemented in the right spirit, since their methods 'tend to crystallise into a system'[36]

The official spirit was willing, but the financing was lacking, even after the issue of the Hadow Report. Without statutory funding there was relatively little increase in numbers – by 1937, only 87 nursery schools were recognised by the Ministry of Education, half of which were run by the voluntary sector.[37]

The Nursery Schools Association (after 1972 the British Association of Early Childhood Education and now Early Education), was founded in 1923 with Margaret McMillan as its first president, and was housed at 29 Tavistock Square on the floor below the Abbatts' flat.[38] The house also contained the Froebel Society and Junior Schools Association, the Child Study Society, the Home and School Council of Great Britain and the New Education Fellowship. It would appear that anyone visiting London on business concerning progressive education would be sure to call there at some point.

By the mid-1930s, the improvement of school designs was a topic of widespread discussion. Oliver Stanley, the President of the Board of Education (equivalent to minister), noted the changes of the previous 15 years as 'a revival of the spirit of humanism', but it still had far to go. In 1935, Lady [Nancy] Astor, the MP for Plymouth Sutton, supported a 'ten year plan' to improve conditions;

'Children who work in dark and airless classrooms', wrote the *Nursery World* editor, 'will not be able to benefit fully from the new physical training schemes'.[39]

Early in 1934, Goldfinger worked in collaboration with the Abbatts to develop a demonstration model of a Nursery School for exhibition by the eponymous Association. After much labour, it was rejected, in Paul Abbatt's words, because 'it does not include sufficient ideas

Northwich Nursery School, 1938. Architects Leslie Martin and Sadie Speight

of Miss De Lissa whom you went to see about it.'[40] This is presumably the same scheme for which Goldfinger drew an attractive coloured perspective, showing the whole of one side of windows folded away, and an indoor sandpit. At the back of the room, a low platform against the wall

has access by a flight of steps and then slides to bring you back to earth. In the foreground, a child is working at a double-sided easel. There is an impression of spaciousness that in reality seems improbable.

In fact, owing to want of capital, most of the schools that opened in the 1930s were not new buildings, but converted houses, such as the Fortis Nursery School run by Beatrix Tudor-Hart, or the Dulwich Nursery, a house converted by the modern architects Godfrey Samuel and Valentine Harding. A rare example of a completely new building was that for Kensal House flats, which the architect Maxwell Fry, in conjunction with Housing Consultant Elizabeth Denby, insisted on including in the Kensal House development by the Gas Light and Coke Company. At Northwich, Cheshire, in 1938, a Quaker benefactress commissioned a lightweight timber school from the architects Leslie Martin (future chief architect of the London County Council) and his wife, Sadie Speight, which had many of the characteristics of post-1945 school buildings.

Nursery and chairs designed by Ernö Goldfinger, with other furniture by Paul and Marjorie Abbatt.
Toys included Horse from *Farm Set*, Camel and Elephant from *Wild Animal Set*, *First Train* and *Peg Board*.
First published in *Decoration* 1935

GOLDFINGER AND ABBATT

After working on the Tavistock Square flat and the Midford Place building, Ernö Goldfinger continued his association with the Abbatts in designing toys and furniture plus their 1936 showroom at 94 Wimpole Street which lasted for the lifetime of the business. Continuing the sequence that began in 1934 at the Dorland Hall, Goldfinger designed the display for 'The Child' section of the British Pavilion in the 1937 Paris Exhibition that lasted for only three months, and another for the MARS Group that was only on view for three weeks. There followed a scheme for a generously sized house for the Abbatts at Ibstone, Buckinghamshire, where they owned a farm with an existing older house. This remained unbuilt owing to the war but instead, after the war, Goldfinger built a modest bungalow on the land for a farmworker.

Perhaps most architects have an interest in childhood as a source of creative energy. This was true of many within the Modern Movement, notably after 1945 when British system-built schools became famous throughout the world. Many architects certainly seem to have preserved a very active 'inner child' into old age. Some special connection must however have sparked between Goldfinger and Paul Abbatt, although their initially playful relationship became stormy at times, as happened with others of his clients.

Paul himself seems to have had some design ability, but was willing to step back and allow Goldfinger to exercise his expertise in the early stages of the business. In 1933 when the collaboration began, the 31-year old architect was living in Paris following his studies at the Ecole des Beaux-Arts. There he had formed part of a breakaway group of students in the mid-1920s who persuaded

Auguste Perret, the leading specialist in designing for concrete construction, to open a teaching studio or Atelier, located in a temporary building, the 'Palais de Bois', originally made for the Paris exhibition of 1925. As its title indicates, this was made of wooden construction, but Goldfinger's enjoyment of wood as a material probably went back to his family's business interests in forestry and sawmills in Transylvania.

Perret remained one of his heroes, but he also enjoyed encounters with the Austrian Adolf Loos, then frequently in Paris, who emphasised the natural textures and markings of marble and wood as contributors to the Modernist aesthetic. Goldfinger also knew the German artist Max Ernst, associated with Surrealism, one of whose techniques involved making rubbings from wood grain ('frottage') and incorporating them in his work. At his house, 2 Willow Road, Hampstead, completed in 1939, Goldfinger lined the walls of the living room with plywood and he and his wife Ursula collected many wooden objects, a selection of which is displayed on the deep window ledge overlooking Hampstead Heath. In addition, they chose to buy a wooden head sculpture by Henry Moore from an exhibition in aid of Russia that they mounted in the house in 1942. All these clues help us to understand how Goldfinger's Abbatt designs fitted into a wider personal concern with modern ways of using one of the oldest materials, and relishing its visual and tactile qualities.

The Abbatt logo

A letter from Goldfinger to Paul Abbatt in November 1933 states 'the drawings of the trade mark are finished. I am having them photographically reduced, in order that you shall have an idea how they will look when used as rubber stamp, letter paper or label for the toy boxes[41]. The device, with a boy and girl in silhouette holding hands, may have been suggested by a French book of 1932 by Nathalie Parain, *Ribambelles*, a term that describes exactly what we see on its cover – figurines cut with scissors from folded paper to make a ribbon-form, published by Flammarion in the children's series, 'Les Albums du Père Castor'. A copy of this book was still among Goldfinger's posessions in his Hampstead house when this passed to the National Trust in the 1990s, making it the likely source of the idea.

In the Goldfinger archive there are drawings showing the adaptation of the device shaped to a roundel in which the figures are the negative cut-out, as executed for a projecting sign to the side of the shop in Wimpole Street. Another sheet contains sketches for posters announcing

Abbatt Logo
designed by
Ernö Goldfinger,
1933

Nathalie Parain
Ribambelles,
Albums du Pere Castor,
1932

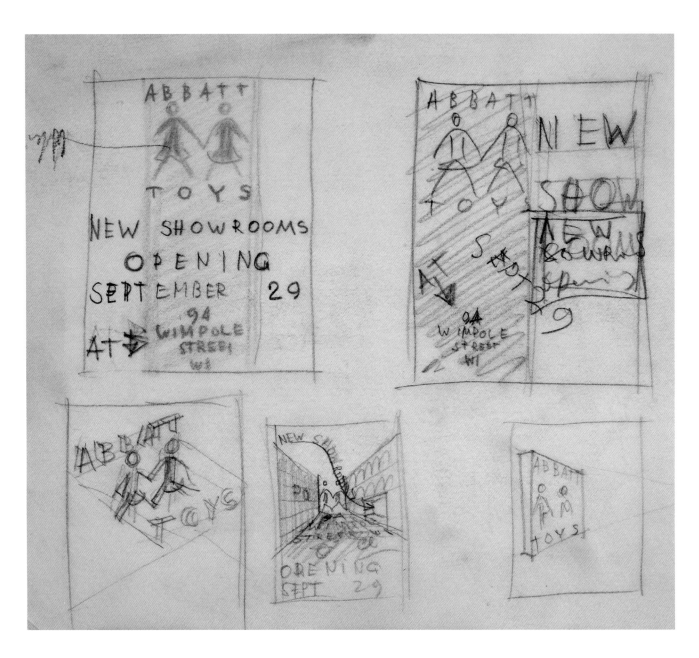

Ernö Goldfinger, studies for posters for the opening of the Abbatt showroom, 1936

the opening on 29 September 1936, probably never developed or printed, one with a simplified perspective looking down the street with a serpentine arrow entering the recess of the shopfront and carrying the words 'New Showrooms'.

Furniture

The cabinet-making facilities set up by the Abbatts made it easy for them to commission furniture on a speculative basis for exhibition displays and for sale. Some examples were shown in the 1934 exhibition at the Dorland Hall, already described, and while no photograph of this can be found, there is a record of an unidentified nursery (p.32), about which Marjorie wrote in *Decoration* magazine, with simple cupboards. A different child's chair, presumably by Goldfinger, features here, made with a metal frame and a plywood seat and back. Like the adult version behind in the photograph and the chromed chairs on a similar model used at home by Goldfinger in Hampstead, it is stackable. The larger ones, at least, were produced as samples while he was in Paris, in the hope that they would be taken up by a manufacturer. The picture (see p.32) was described in Marjorie's article as a small nursery planned for durability and easy cleaning, with the floor made of cork tiling, and the lower part of the walls in thin cork.

The furniture was partly in birch and partly cellulosed in bright colours. The cooker and refridgerator were for the use of the nurse. Without the effect of the colurs, it loses much of its original character.

Furniture ideas continued to develop, and the 1938 Abbatt catalogue illustrates an all-plywood children's chair, described as a 'Posture Chair – perfectly proportioned to the child's figure.'[42] This was a miniature version of an adult model that Goldfinger developed at the same time, with a hinged back in plain plywood and painted sides, and was probably made by Aircraft Ltd.[43] This was shown with a matching 'Growing Table', with a linoleum top (described as white, but clearly not the case with the catalogue photo), and a novelty feature of different sets of the bowed table 'supports' so that the height can be changed to suit the growing child. The appetising colours offered for these are 'red ochre, apple green or sky blue'.

The catalogue entry mentions that Goldfinger 'has also designed for us Unit Bookshelves and Playshelves, which, while suitable for a nursery, are adaptable for use when the child is older.' A forthcoming furniture catalogue is announced, but it seems likely that with the impending war, this was never produced, as no copy has been traced. One of the items was the 'Play trolley', illustrated in a catalogue of 1936, containing 'four differently coloured trays for holding, say, cutting-out things, sewing materials, painting things. The bottom tray is lined with zinc, so could be used for clay or sand. The top is sunk and holds firmly the tray which is in use. The sliding door can be used as a table-top.'

Units of this type, for which miniature versions were made and survive as part of the Goldfinger archive at the RIBA, formed the front of the display, 'The Child' at the Paris exhibition in 1937, linked with boards laid on top. They would have been useful as multipurpose nursery furniture, and the warm pastel-ish colours in the model indicate what the colour schemes might have been like more generally. The other unit has closely-spaced runners instead of shelves, evidently for storage of Abbatt playtrays in their early form with frames surrounding the pictures. On top are Goldfinger's alphabet playtrays and on the floor beneath, shape fitting toys and the 'first train'.

The British Pavilion at the exhibition, designed by Oliver Hill, continued the policy of his two Dorland Hall exhibitions, through the second of which he would have met Goldfinger. Between 1933 and 1937, Hill had become passionate about school design, offering his services free to the Council for Industrial Design (COID) for the design

of a 'model' school in Camberwell, never built. Frank Pick, the vice-chairman of London Underground, was chairman of the COID, established by the Government in the aftermath of the 1933 Dorland Hall show as a promotional vehicle for design and as a research body, and as a subsidiary of the Board of Trade. The design and message of the 1937 Pavilion was its responsibility. Frank Pick was keen to emphasise British values in terms of social stability and quality of life, reflecting the importance of British exports in areas such as sports equipment and clothing, leather goods, ceramics and books. Although criticised for its smug middle-class presentation of a country still riven with problems of industrial stagnation and inequality, the Pavilion won approval from many visitors, a representative of whom, B. M. Ahlberg, wrote to the *Daily Telegraph* describing the Nursery as 'a startling success'.[44]

The section 'The Child', for which Paul Abbatt wrote the short catalogue essay, fitted the theme effectively. Visitors found it in the low-ceilinged lower part of the two-storey building, after going down a big spiral ramp ending in a varied display of farm carts and agricultural tools. Goldfinger was the only architect apart from Hill to be involved in the display design, and was invited by Hill for a weekend at his country retreat, Valewood, near

Haslemere, a strange encounter that he later recalled with humour in an interview.[45] A colour sketch by Goldfinger for the 1937 display shows the dominant pale blue of the sky, used as a background for toy planes. The details in the drawing are only indicative in terms of the final selection of objects, and in the event, only one plane was shown, which was among Goldfinger's designs for Abbatt described in their own catalogue as 'Nursery Airliner in 6 coloured pieces to be assembled. It can be taxied along the floor for a long take-off, but a practical point in its favour, it never flies!'.[46] The corner of the display space is masked by a bent cloud intersecting a sample of a climbing frame in a playfully Constructivist spirit.

Although Abbatt products were visually dominant, the display necessarily included toys and equipment from a range of manufacturers, all listed in the official catalogue with its Ravilious cover. These were still representative of the more high-minded part of the toy trade. On the rear wall were different sizes of Star Yachts – a business started after the First World War in Birkenhead by a Belgian émigré, Franz Denye, and others by Clyde Craft Ltd. For many years, a group of larger yachts was conspicuous on the broad window ledge of the Goldfinger house at 2 Willow Road, Hampstead, ready for action at the Whitestone Pond or the Highgate yacht pond.

The mechanical model boats and trains were supplied by Bassett Lowke of Northampton.[47]

A child-scale set of 'Kitchen cabinet and sink' came from Easiwork Ltd., a thriving company for whom Goldfinger did designs.[48] The remainder of the furniture was by Abbatts, with the carpenter's bench taking pride of place among other practical tools and items of domestic equipment. As Paul Abbatt wrote, 'His nursery presents means to ends, equips him for school and life, makes him resourceful, understanding, confident.'[49]

A prominent feature was the screen on which were mounted enlarged photographs of children by Edith Tudor-Hart (1908-1973), who moved from Vienna to London in 1933 with her English husband, a doctor. She had been a member of the Communist Party and continued to serve it by acting as a link in a spy network for Russia while continuing her profession as a photographer.[50] A letter in Goldfinger's archive adds a little more detail both of the collaboration with Frank Pick and the colours and materials. In the first week of July, Goldfinger met Pick at the Pavilion and as a result sent instructions to the display company, Sage & Co., to change 'the vertical, curved portion of the display platform in the background', from red ochre to slate grey,

Ernö Goldfinger drawing for *The Child* display at British
Pavilion, *Exposition Internationale des Arts et Techniques
dans la Vie Moderne*, Paris, 1937

Photograph of *The Child* display, including photo screen
by Edith Tudor-Hart.

while the sailing boats needed brackets and 'to be strung out according to my design', and finally some additional cork to be stuck to the wall at the back of the miniature kitchen.[51]

There was one further collaboration on an exhibition display, some six months later, when the MARS Group (Modern Architectural Research) succeeded, after much delay owing to shortage of funds, in putting on an exhibition at the New Burlington Galleries near the

Ernö Goldfinger, Nursery section.
Modern Architecture Exhibition
(MARS Group) New Burlington
Galleries 11-29 January 1938

Royal Academy, a space for hire that had housed the International Surrealist Exhibition in 1936 and was to show '20th Century German Art' in July 1938, a deliberate riposte to the Nazis' exhibition of 'degenerate art' the previous year.

The space for the room-set of a nursery, forming an annexe to the main display space reached through the 'Living Room' display, was smaller than in Paris, and the contents therefore rather minimal but as the *Architectural Review* explained, the floor level was raised 'so that the visitor looks at it from the eye-level of the child.'[52] The low cupboard with a double 'tambour' front was almost certainly on loan from Goldfinger himself, and possibly other items too. A sandpit is let into the floor with a panel to cover it, an imaginative idea, and an indoor climbing frame with a rope ladder faced the pretend window. Two of Goldfinger's later plywood child chairs were parked against the back wall while a wooden car and train occupied the floor, with a Kaj Bojesen rocking horse from Denmark at the back. Most remarkable perhaps in the context are the reproductions of old master paintings. The introductory space alongside included a much-enlarged photo of Ursula Goldfinger with Peter, flanked by a chequerboard of smaller images on projecting fins showing nursery schools (readily

identifiable are Kensal House, Dartington and Dulwich). The two low-level cabinets, probably one ones previously shown in Paris, flank the wall.

The magnum opus of Goldfinger for the Abbatts, however, was their shop at 94 Wimpole Street. Their decision to move beyond the rather hidden premises in Midford Place must have demonstrated confidence in the future of the business, and this location served them until Marjorie sold the firm in 1973. There was possibly a rationale in choosing a location in the heart of London's district of medical specialists, where middle class children would be taken for consultations of different kinds and in need of a treat afterwards. It was also not far from some of the leading department stores in Oxford Street. Wigmore Street, a stone's throw away, contained The Times Book Club at No.42 and the shop of Gordon Russell Ltd., representing a 'safe' form of modern design, at No.40, designed in a modern style by Geoffrey Jellicoe and Richard Wilson and opened in 1935.[53]

The row of three shop units, of which Abbatts occupied the ground floor and basement of the middle one, had only recently been put up as an extension to the wholesale operation of the department store Debenham and Freebody, which fronted onto Wigmore Street. The street façade, by the architects Gibson and Gordon, had wide openings to the shops, divided by rusticated stone piers. In the *Architectural Review*, Goldfinger explained the rationale for the design, 'This shop in Wimpole Street, London, is for the sale of nursery equipment, toys, books for children and nursery school outfits for indoors and outdoors, manufactured by the owners. Both small objects, such as toys and books, and large ones, like climbing-frames, swings and furniture, had to find a right place in the show window and shop. The shop is located in a narrow and rather busy street. For this reason the main window was set back 7ft from the building line. This creates a porch, where potential customers can inspect the display of goods at their leisure. Three distinct show windows were made: on the two sides … are shown small objects, books etc., and in the centre, protected by glass going down to the floor, the main show window, which extends in depth if necessary to the back end of the shop and is limited in practice by screens in front of which the objects are displayed. Nearest to the pavement on the two side pillars are arranged cork backgrounds ... for advertisements, prints, etc. Access to the shop is by a plate-glass door without a frame, having only a top and bottom rail and hung on an automatic self-closing pivot. The front of the shop is devoted to the sale of small toys; farther back is the book section.'[54]

Goldfinger's solution was exceptionally elegant, dividing the window horizontally by a rolled steel joist (one of the surviving elements still visible on the exterior) which was structurally redundant, but architecturally effective in proclaiming modernity. Above the clerestory glazing in the upper part of the window, there was a soffit whose front face was framed with a narrow white surround, on top of which the name of the business was displayed in three-dimensional sans-serif letters, also painted white. Below this line, the window was formed of an exceptionally large single sheet of glass. The frameless glass door, swinging two ways, had a tubular chrome steel handle running full height on each side, something that later became commonplace but must have been one of the earliest of its kind. Either side of the window, the 'cheeks' running back from the stone-faced piers contained the additional display windows and circular air-extract vents for the basement below, which had a pavement light and is shown on the plan with three office desks. Inside, the early photographs show a low fitting assembled from cupboard units bridged by boards to create a child-friendly domain clear of the pathway from the door and giving the external window-shopper a good view of the floor, on which toys and furniture are laid out. In the photos, the child chairs are of bent wood, probably supplied by the famous Thonet company. On the table is laid out a road traffic game of

Exterior and interior of the Abbatt showroom,
94 Wimpole Street, at the time of opening, September 1936

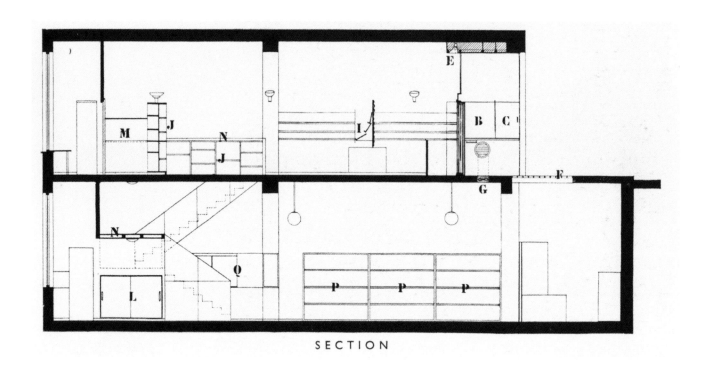

SECTION

Cross-section of ground floor and basement, 94 Wimpole Street. Key: B, show case; C, poster frame; E, soffit lighting; F, pavement lights; G, ventilation; H, lobby; I, display shelves; J, bookcases; K, book display; L, stores; M, packing table; N, display table; O: 6ft by 3ft standard screens; P, shelving for small toys; Q, post-card display element.

some description, featuring many Belisha Beacons, then a novelty still only two years old.

The shop was divided into zones, with the smaller items towards the front and books to the back. The number of these sold seems to have varied over the years, but several book lists were issued before and during the war, at a time when children's picture books were undergoing a revival in Britain. A set of shelves along the right-hand wall provided for the display of the growing range of play-trays and puzzles, and would have brought a strong element of colour into the room.

The shop conveyed more than most the intangible values of the Abbatt brand, including its mild austerity and neatness, in contrast to the profusion more associated with toyshops of all periods. Over time, especially from the mid 1950s, it seems to have become more crowded with stock. Like other designs now regarded as classics of 1930s Modernism, it probably faded into the background and was taken for granted, until for Christmas in 1967, as Fiona MacCarthy noted in the *Guardian*, the Abbatts,

'grandparents of good toyshops … have stripped off the old brown varnish from their pre-war shop … and brightened the place up with a sparkling white display', admitting, as perhaps a design historian in the making ought, that she 'preferred my Abbatt's the worthy dowdy way.'[55]

The ghost of the shopfront remains in the form of the two steel beams across the upper part of the window and the round ventilator grilles in the surviving recess off the pavement. Currently in use as a bar, it is perhaps not beyond hope of reconstruction to its former elegance.

ABBATT TOYS

Catalogue cover by
Madeleine Robinson, c.1934

THE ABBATT TOY RANGE
BEFORE 1939

Describing what Abbatt toys actually were may appear simple. Their regular mail-order catalogues tell us what they sold, but these were a combination of items directly produced by them and others bought in from outside, with the sources of the objects rarely given. Dating these catalogues relies on internal evidence. Those issued from 29 Tavistock Square predate the autumn of 1936, while in one with a pale blue cover, the announcement of a 10-14 day tour of Sweden in May 1939, to be led by Paul Abbatt, BA, 'to find out 'at first hand about the educational system of that country' enables this version to be fixed to 1938.

Only some of the catalogues issued have been available for the present study, so information in this chapter is to some extent conjectural. Even then, it seems that complete certainty about dates of manufacture and sale would not answer all the possible questions.

While some products (probably those made by the Abbatts themselves) endured in the catalogue for decades, others came and went, although it is hard to put them in a correct sequence. Presumably the toys that only appear once were trialled and, if not popular, dropped within the year to be replaced by something else. To add to the confusion, other products appear in promotional photos in the press (such as *The Lady* magazine, where they were given editorial coverage in December in 1935, 1936 and 1939) but not necessarily in the catalogues.

Some of the Abbatts' designs were genuinely original, many were variants on well-known types, as they usually seemed willing to acknowledge. Edward Newmark, a colleague in the 1950s, commented that their originality lay more with the way they marketed their products than with 'the actual basic designs which mostly came

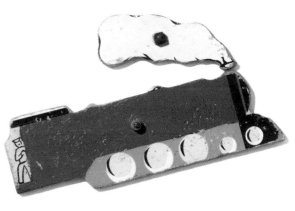

Station picture tray by
Madeleine Robinson, c.1935
(13 x 18 inches)

from old toys already existing or people working in child development, psychology and so on.'[56] More specific information about designers is harder to find, as their names were only credited in some editions of the catalogues. More helpful, if only for a small range of products, is the detailed catalogue of the *Britain Can Make It* exhibition held at the V&A museum in 1946. Here Paul Abbatt's own name appears against several of the simpler items, suggesting that he designed or directed the form of many of the standard products, including those taken from outside inspiration.[57] The Abbatt logo was applied to all their own products, but also put onto others that were licensed for production or retailed by them, which increases the complication of attributing the origin of any individual item carrying the mark.

Wood was almost invariably the material for Abbatt products. Woodcraft Chivalry might have been a clue to this preference, but it had a long tradition in toy making, and as Marjorie explained in 1962, 'it doesn't break, it can take bright colours and is satisfactory for a child to handle and clean-surfaced.'[58] The main alternative for hard objects, which most Abbatt toys were, was metal used as castings or in sheet form, the latter involving a danger of sharp edges. Plastic, its main rival, only became significant in the toy trade after the Second World War.

In order to create some kind of taxonomy, this chapter sorts the toys roughly in terms of the developmental stages that Paul Abbatt was so keen to promote as the speciality of the business. 'Workmanlike toys from the start – valuable experience gained in pleasurable ways' was the heading in one of the earliest catalogues. Alternative forms of this were the *Six Peg Block* and *Form Board*, both used for hammering in wooden pegs.[59] These seem to have been followed by the more versatile *Hammer Pegs*, an H-shaped base with drilled holes, into which coloured cylindrical pegs could be pushed. As the catalogue described it 'Hammer the pegs level with the board, then turn it over and begin again. A splendid outlet for the child's energy and strong enough to withstand the hard knocks of many months.'[60]

In the 1934 catalogue with Madeleine Robinson's cover (p.50), there are *Screw Blocks*, a connector toy (six blocks of different shapes combine in many ways') a *Peg and Block Trolley'*, and a *Peg Mosaic* with different colours to insert in a six-by-six grid of holes. Here too is the *Posting Box*, the idea brought from America, with four holes in the lid of a cubic plywood box, into which the right shape has to be posted. The lid lifts off with a red knob in the middle, and a red tray is supplied to hold the loose parts. Like *Hammer Pegs*, this became a staple product.

Posting Box, a constant in
Abbatt catalogues
from first to last.
(5¼ x 5½ x 5½ inches)

F4

F5

F6

F25

T3

M3

FITTING TOYS

M3 LOOK INSIDE ! Six painted wooden panels to lift out with knobs, disclosing pictures of what is inside. **4/6** (post 6d.)

F4 NEST OF BOXES. These differ from others in their really strong construction, and the good plain colours with which they are painted. **5/11** (post 6d.)

F5 FORM-BOARD. Like the Six-Peg Block, but with triangular and square pegs as well as round ones. Red, yellow and blue. **4/11** (post 6d.)

F6 PEG and BLOCK TROLLEY. Blocks fit on to pegs, which fit on to a trolley. Stained in bright colours and waxed. **3/6** (post 6d.)

F25 ABACUS NUTS. Red, yellow, green and blue "nuts" to screw on to a rod. Pack away into a box with a sliding lid, itself an interesting toy. **4/6** (post 6d.)

F7 POSTING BOX. For posting wooden shapes through corresponding holes. Complete with red tray and three bricks of each shape. **5/11** (post 6d.)

T3 GIANT MATCH-BOX. Giant composition "matches," brightly coloured, in a big strong, coloured, wooden "match-box." Again, the box itself is of interest.
2/6 (post 3d.)

14

F7

2. Running About and Climbing

As the child becomes surer on his feet, he becomes more adventurous. Especially when there is a new baby in the family, he needs to feel that there are compensations for growing up. Anything which adds to his sense of power is welcome. A climbing frame offers him the scope he needs. So does any large material with which he can produce a big effect, such as very big blocks, modelling material in good-sized lumps, sand, hammerpegs, big beads, large crayons.

CLIMBING FRAME

Model B is a compact frame. It incorporates a railed platform with criss-cross sections at two sides and a tower at the corner. Underneath the platform is space for a little den or place to play "house." The bars to the left of the "doorway" are close together and here the baby begins to climb.

Size 1. 2 to 6 years. 14 in. between the rungs. Maximum height 6 ft. 7 in., 4 ft. 3 in. sq. **5½ gns.**

Size 2. 3 to 9 years. 16 in. between the rungs. Maximum height 7 ft. 7 in., 4 ft. 9 in. sq. **6½ gns.**

Carriage and packing 8/-

The Climbing Frame is a child's gymnasium, for use in or out of doors. The town child will play on it with the same joy as the country child plays on trees, barns, hayricks and wagons. Barns and trees may be treacherous, but this toy is made solidly and well, with several good footholds and rods to grasp always within reach. Its use so increases the child's powers and physical control that it greatly adds to his safety. Further, a child who knows how to climb will be released from babyish habits of dependence. The Climbing Frame is built to be left out of doors in all weathers. It is made of specially selected wood, thoroughly coated with a weatherproofing solution. It is delivered in sections, with loose cross-pieces clearly marked, to be screwed to them.

15

Climbing Frame,
25 Best Toys for Each Age,
Abbatt catalogue 1937

The first identifiable catalogue with the Wimpole Street address, is called *Educational Toys* (p.120). Goldfinger may have designed it , with a grey cover and red lettering, using a pattern made up of the Abbatt logo repeated. The layouts push the small photographs to the edge of the pages, an unusual device, probably meant to catch the eye when thumbing through.

In 1937, a new style of catalogue appeared, called *25 Best Toys for each age*, emphasising the Abbatts' concern with guiding buyers to choose toys appropriate to a child's age, although they also acknowledged that children develop at different times.[61] By 1938, in a second version of this, a different and less strictly educational voice is heard through the short descriptions. There are four pages for 'Cradle Days', featuring rattles, soft toy animals with squeaks, and leather animals that 'can be freely sucked and sponged', plus a playpen with its own rug showing a farm wagon and horse. A 'soft doll' has a counterpart with 'ever so cuddly' *Benjamin and Belinda*, a pair of rabbits. Nesting boxes are now cylindrical (blue, red, mauve, green and yellow). *Bagoblox* has 'assorted bricks stained and polished in bright colours. Each one is a treasure to the baby, who gets much amusement simply emptying and filling the bag'. For the early years there were a number of practical items of equipment rather than toys, billed as 'things making for

wellbeing' in 1938. These included the '*Baby Buffer* – the best-designed little car of the kind that we know', and, as *The Lady* remarked, 'strapped into his little low car, the baby can yet reach a toy dropped on the floor without yelling for his Nannie.'[62] This appears to be the same product as the *Little Buffer* made by The Baby Scooter Car Co. of Kentish Town, advertised in *Nursery World*, December 5, 1934. Toys also came on wheels, including the ride-on *Dobbin Push Horse* – 'like a real carthorse', combining realism with a steel chassis and pushing handle.

Ernö Goldfinger designed the *First Train* early in his association with Abbatts, distinguished by not having any wheels and apparently adapted from the American *Floor Train* by the Playskool Institute, about which they heard from their American friend, Mrs Franklin.[63] The catalogue text was persuasive in its advocacy of abstraction, '"First", because so solid and the linking so easy. No wheels to come off or to obscure the simple pattern. For children from two to five this train approaches the ideal of a simple and effective plaything.' It was 'well-finished in five colours', but actual surviving examples of it seem vanishingly rare. There were six pieces, with a locomotive, tender, three open wagons and a guard's van. The joints were made with a toggle on a slanted neck fitting into a corresponding slot, allowing the train to turn on a curve.

A 1939 illustration suggests that the design was further developed with sorting-toy items to put in the appropriate wagon. 'A toy which the very young will love putting together' commented *The Lady*.[64] Later came the *Hitch Train*, similar in appearance but with a different coupling system and a longer-bodied locomotive that 'gives the impression of the power and streamline of modern rail transport.'[65]

Locking Letters, designed by Freda Skinner, used the same jointing system.[66] According to the catalogue entry, it was deliberately planned to lead children unconsciously into literacy, 'First and foremost a delightful and solid toy for locking into chains and trains, but the child naturally learns the alphabet using it.'[67] This item carried on for years, but became more didactic with more letters and a less decorative appearance. Skinner may also have been the designer of the *Number Tray*. In the earliest versions, the zero, which is a fixed part of the frame, was placed after the figure nine, but later more logically moved ahead of the one - a single piece, with every successive numeral cut into the appropriate number of pieces. Beneath each numeral are the appropriate number of objects in a matching colour (leaves, eggs, chicks, etc). *Alphabet Insets*, a set of capitals designed by Goldfinger, was joined by a matching lower-case alphabet and a set of plain numerals. 'To build

yourself – motor-cars, a railway and a ferry boat', the catalogue recommended the *B12 Transport Set*, for £1/19/6 (a snip below £2), a set of beechwood blocks and wheels from which all these items could be assembled.

One of their longest-lasting products was wooden bricks. There was nothing original about the concept, for wooden building bricks were a nineteenth century nursery staple, supplied neatly packed in boxes with wooden lids covered with a printed and stencil-coloured picture. These were usually a mixture of plain shapes and some fancy ones, which might even have pieces of metal foil paper stuck onto them.

The Abbatts' 1932 exhibition included 'boxes of large bricks from the Pestalozzi-Froebel House in Berlin. These were not toy building-bricks as we had previously thought of them, but solid worthwhile objects for child use.' The contrast intended here may have been with the well-established stone bricks, originally from Germany and later made by Lotts in England, with their realistic details and small component parts. Through most of the lifetime of the Abbatt firm, several alternative types of building bricks were supplied as choices, such as the *Nest of Bricks*, an idea seen at the Leipzig toy fair, 'as used by quite little children, each box of a clear lovely colour and very strongly made.'

LETTERS AND NUMBERS

R1 NUMBER TRAY. Each numeral is cut into the number of pieces that it represents. Below each is painted (in the same colour) a corresponding number of objects.
7/6 (post 7d.)

R16 HAMMERNAIL ALPHABET. Little children take a great delight in hammering. Nail mosaic has been second to none of our toys in popularity and this new nail mosaic with clear capital letters on the shiny tiles offers many new possibilities. Children love to "make words" before they can write. 5/11 (post 6d.)

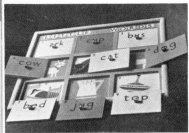

R6 LITTLE WORDS. Soon learnt, for they lift out by means of little knobs and disclose the appropriate picture underneath. 4/6 (post 6d.)

R12 NUMBER INSETS. Numbers, 2½ in. high, fit into a board which is thinner than themselves, so that they stand out in relief and are easily picked out. 3/6 (post 6d.)

R9 ALPHABET INSETS. These well-designed letters, 2½ in. high, fit into a board which is thinner than themselves, so that they stand out in relief and are easily picked out. Children readily become familiar with the shapes of the letters in playing with them and fitting them in. Lacquered and framed. 7/6 (post 8d.)

R10 ALPHABET. The letters separate, with ten extra of the more usual in a box. 2/11 (post 3d.)

R13 NUMBERS, one to five, in a box, two of each. 1/- (post 3d.); one to ten, 1/- (post 3d.)

R2 LOCKING LETTERS. Painted on solid blocks of wood which interlock in the same way as do the trucks of the First Train. The letters can be joined together, and when the word has been formed, it can be played with as a single unit. The lengths of different words and their construction can be gauged by the little child, and impressed on his mind by handling and playing with this new alphabet. 26 letters, with extra a, e, i, o, b, d, f, i, s, t, in a wooden box. 21/- (post 1/-)

R14 SCRIPT ALPHABET INSETS. A new alphabet to go with the capitals above. The tall letters are 2½ in. high. 7/6 (post 8d.)

R15 SCRIPT ALPHABET. Thirty-six script letters in a box.
2/11 (post 3d.)

32

Letters and Numbers.
25 Best Toys for Each Age,
Abbatt catalogue 1938

These thin-walled cubes with one open side would slide into one another and be stored compactly, and could then be taken out and pile up as a tower.

Prior to the Abbatt's launch, Margaret Lowenfeld had adopted as a central part of her therapeutic repertory the large, solid beech-wood bricks described in detail by the novelist H. G. Wells, in his book *Floor Games*, 1911, illustrated by photographs of various models made with them, peopled by toy soldiers and 'natives', all of a strikingly Imperialist character. Wells never worked with any manufacturer, but gave dimensions for the modular series of bricks, including some cut with curves, recommending that a local carpenter be instructed to make them, together with plain boards that could be used for floors and roofs. Even by the 1930s, the 'local carpenter' might no longer be available for such a task, or otherwise the parent or teacher might not have spared the time, so the Abbatts were canny to provide for their needs. One of the earlier Abbatt catalogues illustrates two boys making an elaborate Wellsian tableau 'completed by twigs from the garden and little wooden toys.'[68] At this point, the bricks were sold in a box, like Richter and earlier types, but later they were offered in tough canvas kitbags with eyelet holes around the top and a string to tie them up.
The plainness of the actual bricks did not deter

imagination, but quite the opposite. In *Intellectual Growth in Young Children*, Susan Isaacs had reported that at the Malting House, 'building with ordinary wooden bricks was very frequent – houses, bridges, the Cambridge Colleges, the Tower of London, tunnels, castles and so on.'[69] The Abbatts always emphasised the need for enough bricks to build adventurous creations.

As glowingly described in an early catalogue, 'H. G. Wells box of bricks forms a rich supply of building material for the child who wants plenty. It is not a minimum quantity got up to look like an adequate present; it is a rich mine of material from which the child can draw until he has built his houses, shops, factories to the limits of his imagination.'[70] In 1970, the adoption of this design and its merits are more fully explained, 'Of all the playthings we can provide, for most children bricks last longest in interest. When we started in business, bricks were small and fiddly and we were immediately asked for something larger. We bought from Woolworths some plain wood legs meant for small tables and sawed them into different lengths. A better idea was H. G. Wells's, who commissioned the village carpenter to make some bricks identical to those we now present, plain and relating to one another in size, with some flat pieces for floors and roofs. We still think they are the best for they can

H.G. Wells Bricks, sold by
Abbatt from 1933

represent anything a child dreams up – roads, fences, and even trains – and later, quite a Wates-looking building [a reference to a then-flourishing developer of middle-class modern housing]. Used in conjunction with little animals, vehicles, houses, people, they give plenty of scope for imaginative play. A bag of bricks provides more different shapes, which lend themselves to making buildings. Some may find this more interesting – more classical perhaps?'[71]

The Wells bricks were too large for very small hands, and for years one to four, there was *First Building Bricks*, described as 'solid cubes of wood, some cut diagonally, with long slats'. These were stained and coloured and supplied in a 'strong wooden box'.[72] They were included (with the same photograph and text as the Abbatt catalogues) in the catalogue of the Army and Navy Stores.[73]

Another wooden construction toy found in the earlier catalogues was *Matador*, the creation of the Austrian engineer, Johann Korbuly in 1899 and still in current production. Very likely, this was seen by the Abbatts in Vienna and then imported – 'makes models which really work. No nuts or bolts, very easy to use: attractively coloured and well-fitting'. The wheeled vehicles or aeroplanes made with *Matador* would have been

compatible with the Wells bricks. In 1939, perhaps only briefly owing to the war, a *Screwso* aeroplane on a similar principle to *Matador* was offered, producing a pleasingly anachronistic biplane with pilot and passenger.[74] *Matador*, as a post-war catalogue explained, 'was suitable for a wide age-range, for while construction is very easy and working diagrams clear, quite complicated working models can be made.'[75] The Abbatts recognised the value of the much more famous and enduring *Meccano*, but were also careful to warn parents not to give it to children who had not developed the necessary dexterity. *Matador* worked the same way, as did other wooden construction toys like *Tinkertoy* (not seen in Abbatt catalogues), and after the war, *Matador* was joined by *Connector*.

Equipment for outdoor play was an Abbatt speciality. The 'Jungle gym' was an American invention in 1920 by the lawyer Sebastian Hinton who was obsessed by the idea of 'monkey instinct' in children and trademarked the name which while becoming generic, may also have prompted the use of the alternatives 'Climbing Frame' (as used by the Abbatts) or 'monkey bars' for similar products.[76] In *The Nursery World*, Susan Isaacs described a variety of climbing devices, see-saws etc., and also 'the climbing frame' which along with ladders and other items 'are best made by a local carpenter or ladder-maker', since this would be

H G Wells Bricks 'an unending interest', from 1938 catalogue,
25 Best Toys for Each Age

cheaper than those bought from 'any educational supply firm'. Isaacs continued, 'with such a frame or cage, a group of small children will play most happily for long periods – climbing up and down, stretching their arms and taking the weight of their bodies off their legs … hanging upside down and in all positions, and in general getting splendid exercise as well as lots of fun; and sometimes turning the whole thing into a house or cubby-hole, with rugs and cushions, for make-believe play.'[77]

This confirms that the Abbatts were not the first to offer such a product, but its constant appearance in their catalogues indicates that it was a good seller. 'Children always will be climbing', declares the sales blurb in a mid-1930s catalogue, 'and it is a good thing that they should, for so is surefootedness developed and a healthy fearlessness. Here is something really safe to climb on, indoors or out.' The frame was delivered in a flat pack but 'stoutly built in sections which screw easily together'. Where it would have been cheaper to have one made locally is hard to determine, but at nearly six pounds for

Nursery Slide, attributed to
Ernö Goldfinger, made from
1933. Advertisement from
Vogue, 1937

the smaller size and seven for the larger, it was among the most expensive item in the catalogue.

Slides came in different sizes too. The smallest being suitable for indoor use, as demonstrated in a piece of home-movie footage taken by Ernö Goldfinger of small children in party clothes being shot down it with delight.[78] The basic Abbatt slide came in three separate parts – steps, platform and slide. A dual-purpose variant was the *Cupboard Slide* which 'makes a storeplace for big toys as well as a slide. The steps and slide fit right underneath when not in use.' This was not all, however, since 'The platform [with handrails for safety] forms a bus or ship to occupy several children in imaginative play.'[79] Later, around 1938, came the *Abbatt Nursery Chute* to meet a demand for an intermediate size (four feet or 1.21m in height) between the *Nursery Slide* and 'the big *Abbatt Chute* for out of doors'.[80] In the 1950 catalogue, it is shown with tubular steel steps and support, no doubt owing to the timber shortage.

The third main category of outdoor equipment was for sand play, something children have probably always engaged in. The chronicler Giraldus Cambrensis writes about building sandcastles (or, in his case, monasteries) as a child on the sands at Manorbier in Wales in the mid-twelfth century.

A sandpit was among the play amenities at the Passmore Edwards Settlement in Bloomsbury in the early 1900s (now known as Mary Ward House). 'A sand-pile in a sunny corner can be looked upon as a necessity of childhood' wrote Susan Isaacs.[81] It might be thought that it was hard to sell products for this activity, apart from wooden spades and sieves, but a 'sandset' designed by Educational Playthings Inc. of New York was offered in 1938, with buckets and a sieve trolley. For the sand itself, pre-war Abbatts offered a moveable sandpit, 'so that children can really get into it and have the pleasure of standing in the sand and shovelling it about.' It was lined with zinc, so that it could be 'used for paddling in the summer and for sailing boats.' The shallow box, three feet square, with hinged lids that made flat surfaces, could be picked up and moved across a lawn or terrace. The idea originated from an enquiry from a Bloomsbury neighbour in Gordon Square, for whom a prototype was made so that a group of children living locally could play together.[82] In 1963, they described what made sand such a good play material. 'It can be made and destroyed. The feel of it trickling through your fingers is very sensuous, even wet sand.'[83]

Betty Bashall already offered a similar product, but while the Abbatt version was in plain plywood, hers was painted 'jade and yellow with a striped orange canopy', which

probably says much about the different cultures of taste to which each company appealed. Kiddicraft had a much plainer product without the lid or lining, in three sizes, the equivalent to the Abbatt offer being about a quarter of their price of 89/6 or £4/9/6. A sand table, often found in nursery schools, was also available from Abbats.

Also available for group play was the *Playhouse*, built of plywood as a three-sided folding screen, four feet square, 'a splendid centre for housekeeping play and also for playing at "shops," for a flap at one side lets down to make a counter.'[84] (p.71) There was a proper hinged door with a handle. As the catalogue states suggestively, the inside was 'purposely left plain: as the children grow older they will delight in decorating the inside, making curtains, adding a name for the house, windowboxes, etc.'

A more elaborate form of outdoor playhouse or classroom for nursery schools was designed for the Abbatts by Franz Singer, including an upper deck reached by an external stair. A photograph shows Abbatt puzzles and other recognisable items in the shadowy interior, thus identifying it as their product, but it may only have been a one-off trial, as it never appeared in any catalogue. The Puppet Theatre caught the spirit of a puppet revival in the later 1930s, intended for operation by two children in a decorated proscenium to stand on a table, equipped with glove puppet sets for performing versions of *Three Little Pigs* and the Mad Tea Party from *Alice in Wonderland*.

Early on, the Abbatts took the idea of a double-sided easel from Dartington School, although a single-sided version was also available. Slightly older children could use the work bench, attuned to Susan Isaacs' insistence on doing real work with real tools. Measuring two by three feet, it was described as 'enormously strong and solid', and sets of tools graded according to safety were supplied.

Rocking horses were a staple of the toy trade, but while offering a very simple small-scale example, Abbatts promoted in its place the *Fun-boat* – 'Lighter, cheaper and more portable than a rocking-horse or see-saw, the *Fun-boat* is a safe toy which promotes fun and friendship. See how near the ground the children are, but what a happy time they enjoy.'[85] Two different colour choices were offered, red frame and blue seats or green frame and orange seats. There is an undocumented rumour that it was designed by Oliver Hill, and an example appears in the foreground of a photograph of his single executed Modernist school, at Whitwood Mere, near Castleford, South Yorkshire.[86] The *Funboat* (soon amalgamated to a single word) was another enduring staple for the business,

Franz Singer, *Play House* prototype, c.1938

Horse jigsaw, painted plywood with frame, designed by
Freda Skinner, made from 1934 onwards
(9½ x 11½ inches)

Fire-Engine jigsaw, painted plywood
with frame, designed by Madeleine
Robinson, from 1937
(9½ x 11½ inches)

Motor-Coach jigsaw, painted
plywood with frame, probably by
Freda Skinner, from 1936
(9½ x 11½ inches)

although later James Galt & Co. produced an alternative version, identical but for the addition of a 'safety bar' projecting behind the seats to prevent total nosedive capsize. This despite Abbatts' claim that their model did not tip over, and the unlikelihood of it having continued on sale had accidents been at all common, even in such pre-safety conscious times.

Shorter-lived was the *Rowboat*, with real oars and rowlocks, but an open footwell for propulsion along the floor. Although at two and a half feet (0.76m) it was claimed to take two children, the fact of rowing one way and facing the other must have diminished the pleasure with no corresponding gain.[87] Apart from the *Tan-Sad Pedalkar* tricycle (made in Birmingham), wheeled toys to ride on were not a speciality, but the 1937 and 1938 catalogues included the *Flexy Racer* – 'A really grand coaster from America', made by S. L. Allen of Philadelphia, as a companion to the *Flexible Flyer* sledge with steering. The user lay down head first and steered with handles extending the front axle, fitted with 'powerful brakes operated by merely twisting the steering bar'. This was the same year that the product, in production for a further 30 years, was patented, but it seems only to have appeared once in Abbatts' catalogue.

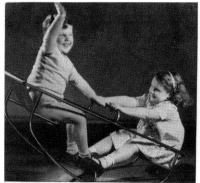

FUNBOAT

G12 **FUNBOAT**. Lighter, cheaper, and more portable than a rocking-horse or see-saw, the Funboat is a safe toy which will not tip over—a toy which promotes fun and friendship. Tubular steel and canvas, red and blue, or green and orange.
27/6 (carriage 1/9)

ROWBOAT

The oars are on swivels which allow just the motion of real sculling. You can move along, too, for the boat has no bottom, and when you push with your feet, it glides along or even shoots along! 2 feet 6 inches long, it will accommodate two very small passengers of three or one larger of five. Enamelled green, with extra strong castors and swivels. **21/-** (carriage 2/-)

24

Funboat and *Rowboat* from 1938 catalogue
25 Best Toys for Each Age

TO THOSE WHO ARE STOCKING THEIR TOY-CUPBOARD

G12 FUNBOAT.
Lighter, cheaper, and more portable than a rocking-horse or see-saw, the Funboat is a safe toy which will not tip over—a toy which promotes fun and friendship. Tubular steel and canvas, red and blue, or green and orange.

27/6 (carriage 1/9)

IN these days, when we are stocking up our store cupboards, we think rather more than usual in terms of food values. What are the body's needs? What kinds of food does it require and how much?

Have you ever thought of toys in terms of their play value?
This is our main consideration in presenting to you these toys—what are the child's play needs?—how long will each toy satisfy not only the present, but the *changing* need? For play is the great developer of his mind and skill and as he develops he requires new possibilities for play.
The baby under a year old is learning to recognise objects by their colour, taste, feel, smell. He requires things to play with which shall be as varied as possible in their shape, weight, texture and in the noise they make when they are moved. When he is about a year old he becomes interested in the relations of the parts to the whole. He likes

toys with large and simple parts which can be taken apart and put together again.
This interest of fitting things together, presently of building, is one which goes on developing through life and is the basis of all the crafts. So it is a mistake to "show how" or make a child copy set patterns. The toy was made for the child, not the child for the toy. Abbatt Toys are devised to be played with in a variety of ways. Further, a toy must be so strongly made that, given reasonable care, it does not break, causing frustration and disappointment.
Lastly, the toy must be well-designed. If we wish a child to acquire a taste for what is beautiful, we do not suffer him to play with anything crude and ugly. Those who know Abbatt Toys will realise the attention paid to strength and durability, to design and colour.

PLAYHOUSE. A splendid centre for housekeeping play and also for playing at "shops," for a flap at one side lets down to make a counter. Substantially built of plywood, varnished on the outside and with painted door and window-frames. Purposely left plain: as the children grow older they will delight in decorating the inside, making curtains, etc. Stands 4 ft. high by 4 ft. wide each way and folds flat. 3 sides, **79/6**; 2 sides, **59/6** (carriage forward).

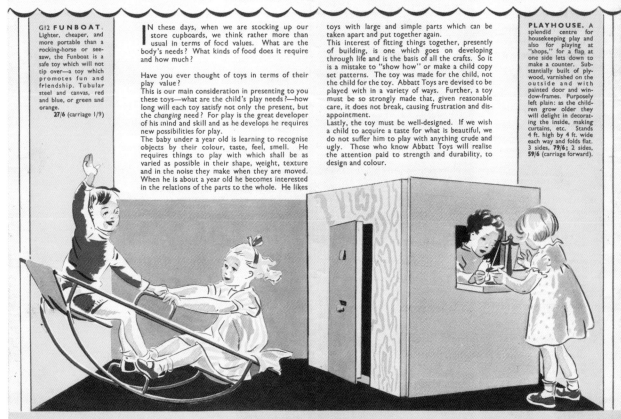

For further notes on the child's development through play see full catalogue of Abbatt Toys

'To those who are stocking
their toy-cupboard',
Abbatt catalogue, 1940

Freda Skinner

While many of the Abbatt toys were non-pictorial, the range did include simple cut-out painted wooden animals in a *Wild Animal Set* and a *Farm Set*. These were designs by Freda Skinner (1911-1993), one of only two designers of the early Abbatt years whose work was identified (sporadically) and whose later career can be traced in some detail. She studied sculpture at the Royal College of Art relatively young, from 1928 to 1930, her fees supported by neighbours of her farming parents in Surrey, including Arthur Rackham and the artist sisters Ethel and Sibyl Pye. Her tutors included Henry Moore, a recent graduate of the college, and Alan Durst.[88] According to Jude Welton, she worked for the Abbatts between 1932 and 1935.[89] She later taught toy making and sculpture at Kingston School of Art, directed the making of three-dimensional landscape maps during the war and became head of Sculpture at Wimbledon School of Art, where her students included William Pye. Her sculptures were commissioned for a number of churches, and she was adventurous in her choice of media.

The Abbatt work for which Freda Skinner is best remembered was for the jigsaw puzzles. These were not the conventional kind, but what were later termed 'play trays'.

The idea for these came from a visit by the Abbatts to the Nursery School at Dartington Hall in Devon, another centre of progressive practice, in 1933, where some one-off examples, presumably made in the estate workshops, were being used. As Jude Welton writes, presumably from what Marjorie Abbatt told her, 'the background sometimes contained an appropriate scene into which the image fitted, and because this was solid, the jig-saw did not fall to pieces, but could be carried around and "shown off".'[90]

It was a simple but effective device that endured through the whole lifetime of the Abbatt business, with some of Skinner's designs, such as the carthorse and bus, still going strong in 1970, amid others using the same technique. They were marketed as superior because other wooden jigsaws had pictures on paper pasted on and liable to scuff or peel. 'Colours are bright, fast and washable', as the 1938 catalogue explained. Some of Skinner's designs for these items have survived in the V&A, showing how she designed them on paper.[91] The puzzles are a sandwich of two layers, with ply on top and usually hardboard below. The early examples (pre-1939) also had an upstand frame around the edge. The pieces look as if they were cut out of the same sheet of plywood as the surround, about 4mm thick and so robust and easy to handle. In fact, the background negative shape could not have produced

Bus jigsaw painted plywood with frame, by Freda Skinner, from 1934
(9½ x 11½ inches)

Motor jigsaw, painted plywood,
by Freda Skinner, from 1934
(7 x 12 inches)

a positive for the pieces without some intervening drill-hole for the saw blade, so the pieces were probably cut separately. The painting is all flat colour in the manner of posters at the time, and was applied by hand, presumably using stencils where necessary. Some details appear to be freehand, however, and they became increasingly skimped through the decades. Skinner's subjects are divided between animals (horse, lamb, cow, tiger and others), and transport (liner, locomotive, car, motor coach and double-decker bus). Her sculptor's training comes across in their three-dimensionability. Human details are applied sparingly, although the sleek red limousine with black running boards and silver hubcaps contains a severe-looking lady passenger, possibly reminiscent of Marjorie's mother, instructing her impassive capped chauffeur from the back seat as they motor through a hilly landscape under a green sky.

Madeleine Robinson

While Skinner seems to have designed the majority of the jigsaws, and sometimes even got her name on them, the Fire Engine, The Zoo and a delightful black terrier with a yellow collar are the work of Madeleine Robinson (1908-1991). A niece of William Heath Robinson, one of three artist brothers, Madeleine was a popular child actress before becoming a student at St Martin's School of Art and the Royal Academy. In 1931, she won the painting scholarship at the British School at Rome, the second woman to do so, with a canal scene that The Times described as 'remarkably well-organised in form, colour and tone.' She returned from Rome in 1934 and her main work for the Abbatts, for puzzles and picture trays began immediately, together with attractive children's picture prints (16 by 14 inches), based on cut paper originals.

The 'picture tray' was adapted from the Montessori idea of 'insets', which are simple coloured shapes with a peg handle in the centre, and matching holes. In a 1962 interview, Marjorie Abbatt explained 'these trays are found very helpful in nursery schools as they encourage children to enlarge their vocabulary and discover which objects belong in which context.'[92] The picture trays have pieces that lift out with a small peg to grasp them, and can then be used like cut-out characters or props in a story-telling game – 'for little children of two and upwards, not only is there a fascination in fitting the pieces in place, but each piece makes a separate toy, which will be used in all kinds of imaginative ways. Older children will use them to draw round.'[93] Eight subjects were in the catalogue pre-war: Station, Haymakers, Street, Beach and Zoo. In early versions, the bus in the street scene has 'General' on it,

Street picture tray, painted plywood,
by Madeleine Robinson, from 1936
(13 x 18 inches)

for the London General Omnibus Company, which was absorbed into the London Passenger Transport Board (London Transport for short) in 1933, so was already an anachronism. The picture trays developed a further level of sophistication as *Stand-Up Jigsaws*, with the pieces fitted into a plain sheet of wood, beneath which was a painted scene (*Pond* or *Nursery School*) which they could then inhabit. More adventurous still was the *Circus*, with 'a flying trapeze which can be set up and a whole circus troupe to put through their antics'.[94] The range was extended in the 1960s with other artists, although some of the earliest designs carried on into the 1970s.

Zoo picture tray, painted plywood, by Madeleine Robinson, from 1936 (13 x 18 inches)

James Gardner

Just before the Second World War, the Abbatts commissioned a rising young designer James Gardner (1907-1995) to design a picture tray with a difference, the *Zoo Zag*.[95] This operated as a simple jigsaw, with the added bonus that the name of the animal was underneath each piece and was an effortless way of starting word recognition and reading. For older children there was the option to play a domino-style game with the pieces. The depiction of London Zoo, then enjoying extra popularity through new buildings such as Berthold Lubetkin's Penguin Pool, was so far as possible correct in terms of the layout.[96] *Zoo Zag* was issued in a box with the rules of the game pasted on the lid. The elaboration of the drawing must have meant that it could not be hand-painted, and was possibly silk-screen printed. The colours became softer in post-war versions.

Gardner's name always appears on *Zoo Zag*, and also on *Airplane Snakes and Ladders*, a board game with 'aeroplanes, gliders, dirigibles, parachutes and other aircraft.'[97] The alarming aspect is that by landing on a 'snake', the player's craft plummets towards the bottom of the board, without ever crashing. However, after the Hindenberg and R101 disasters, the dirigibles, at least,

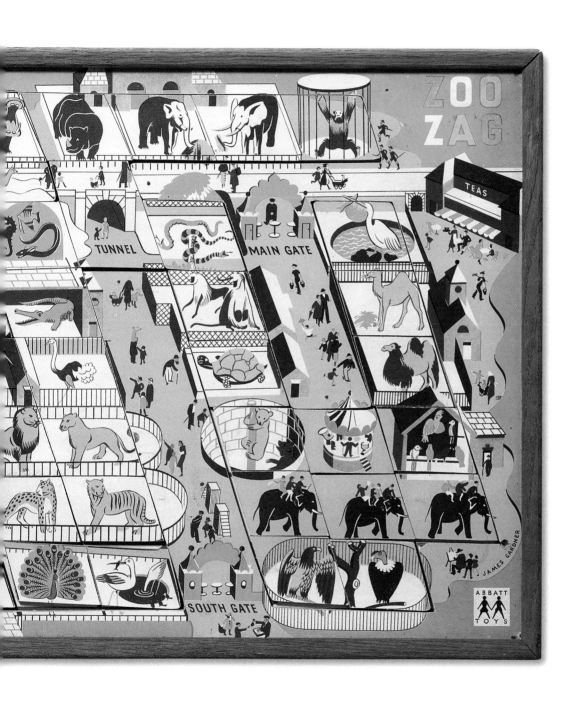

Zoo Zag,
screen-printed
plywood, by James
Gardner, from 1938
(13 x 18 inches)

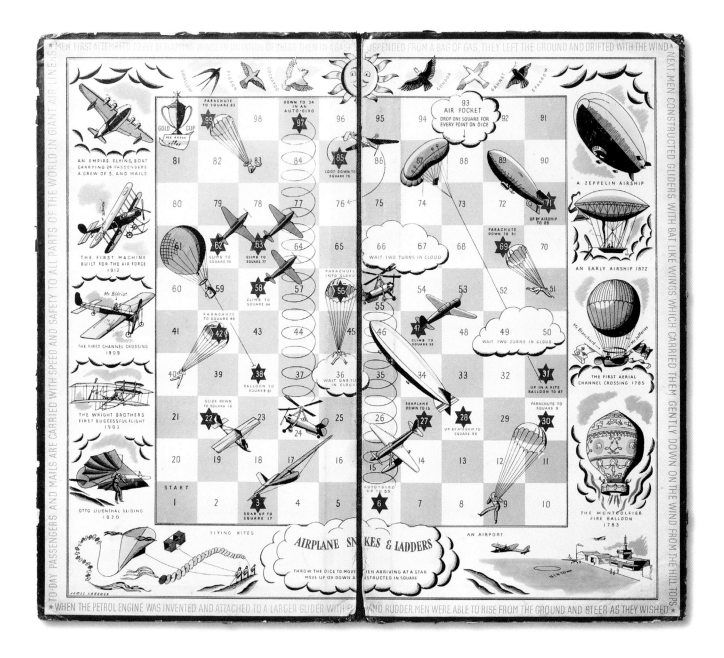

Airplane Snakes & Ladders, printed paper on board, James Gardner, from 1938

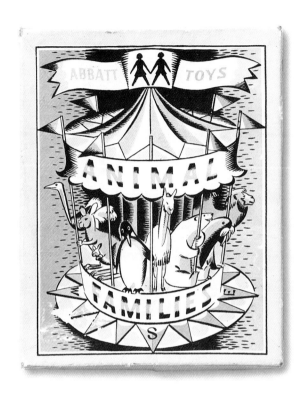

Animal Families, box lid attributed to James Gardner, from 1938; *Snap!*, artist unknown

seem rather ill-omened. His style seems also to match the box lid design for *Animal Families*, a game on the lines of 'Happy Families' issued soon after the war and Gardner may well have designed the cards inside.

The first 'very attractively designed new snap cards', seen in the 1938 catalogue, unfortunately have no named artist. The images have simplicity but also a degree of subtlety in their colour combinations. The box lid has an

SEAL
SLEIGH DOG — PUFFIN — POLAR BEAR

RUSSET DEER
GOLDEN EAGLE — FOX — BADGER

PUFFIN
SEAL — SLEIGH DOG — POLAR BEAR

KOALA BEAR
KIWI — PLATYPUS — KANGAROO

OSTRICH
HIPPOPOTAMUS
GORILLA — AFRICAN ELEPHANT

PEACOCK
CAMEL — IBEX — VULTURE

MOOSE
BEAVER — BISON — BLACK BEAR

PLATYPUS
KOALA BEAR — KIWI — KANGAROO

SLEIGH DOG
SEAL — PUFFIN — POLAR BEAR

DOMESTIC PIG
DOMESTIC SHEEP — COW — HEN

COW
DOMESTIC SHEEP
DOMESTIC PIG — HEN

TIGER
INDIAN ELEPHANT
INDIAN OXEN — CROCODILE

Animal Families, probably by James Gardner

...BEX

BROWN BEAR
MARCO POLO'S SHEEP
WILD HORSE — WOLF

POLAR BEAR
SEAL — SLEIGH DOG — PUFFIN

CROCODILE
INDIAN ELEPHANT
TIGER — INDIAN OXEN

KING PENGUIN
WHALE — WALRUS — ALBATROSS

...HANT

BEAVER
MOOSE — BISON — BLACK BEAR

DOMESTIC SHEEP
DOMESTIC PIG — COW — HEN

INDIAN ELEPHANT
TIGER
INDIAN OXEN — CROCODILE

BISON
BLACK BEAR — MOOSE — BEAVER

...AGLE
...SSET DEER

KANGAROO
KOALA BEAR — KIWI — PLATYPUS

HIPPOPOTAMUS
OSTRICH
GORILLA — AFRICAN ELEPHANT

MARCO POLO'S SHEEP
WILD HORSE — BROWN BEAR — WOLF

BADGER
RUSSET DEER — GOLDEN EAGLE — FOX

Eastern European folk-art flavour. *Picture Dominoes* takes representation of leaves and flowers to greater simplicity.

The range of wheeled toys expanded by the end of the 1930s, marketed individually or as a *Transport Set* of cars, trains and a ferry boat, shown in the catalogue arriving at a terminal made with *H. G. Wells' Bricks*. An alternative was the *Screwso Constructional Set*, with interchangeable parts to make a range of vehicles. 'This big constructional material is such as to afford little children great satisfaction for, by the simplest possible means, quite large and realistic wheel toys can be made. The parts fit easily and are fixed together by means of big wooden nuts and bolts. Each wagon measures 10 inches in length, and is provided with smiling passengers who "stay put," for their seats are holes.' These turned wooden figures with spherical heads are the type much used by Escor Toys, a company founded in Bournemouth in 1938 by Edward Seaton Corner, a former tea planter in India (whose name is contracted in their title), later joined by members of his family.[98] After diverting into military tasks during the war, the company's products became a long-term staple of the Abbatt stock, identified by name in some of their catalogues.

The last page of the 1938 catalogue has a poignant story to tell. Under the heading 'Home-Made Orchestra', it announces that 'Mr. Mack holds classes in the making of simple musical instruments for both indoor and outdoor use. The instruments are harmonious and have an individual and genuine quality sometimes absent from commercial products.'[99] 'Mr. Mack' was in fact the former Bauhaus student and teacher, Ludwig Hirschfeld-Mack (1893-1965), who came to England in 1935, taking work where he could find it. His passion was to coordinate sound and the visual senses, and his teaching in England, at Dartington, Peckham Health Centre and Dulwich Preparatory School, involved the making of simple percussion and woodwind instruments and guidance in improvising with them. The arrangement was the subject of a letter from the Abbatts on 5 December, 1938, offering royalty payments and facilities for holding classes.[100] Advertised as 4-6 on Wednesday afternoons and 'in other localities by special arrangement', did they ever take place?

HOME-MADE ORCHESTRA

Mr. Mack holds classes in the making of simple musical instruments for both indoor and outdoor use. The instruments are harmonious and have an individual and genuine quality sometimes absent from commercial products. Ear and hand are together educated in making them. The table below shows at what age children can make and play the various instruments.

(Classes Wednesdays 4—6. One guinea for four two-hour classes. Children's classes or classes in other localities by special arrangement.)

MUSICAL INSTRUMENTS FOR CHILDREN TO MAKE

Age	Melody Instrument	Motive Instrument (Several tuned tones)	Bourdon Instrument (One tuned tone only)	Rhythmical Instrument (Untuned)
3—5	Singing Tube Mirliton			Stone Stick Rattles: Wooden, Tin Hand Drums: Wooden box, Tin box
5—10	Singing Tube Mirliton Stone Play (8 tones) Xylophone (5-8 tones) (Without resonance box)	2 Stones 2 Sticks Cuckoo Whistle	1 Stone 1 Stick 1 Tone Whistle	Stone Stick Rattle-straw: Wooden, Tin Hand drums: Wooden box, Tin box Wrist Rattles

MUSICAL INSTRUMENTS FOR CHILDREN TO PLAY

Age	Melody Instrument	Motive Instrument (Several tuned tones)	Bourdon Instrument (One tuned tone only)	Rhythmical Instrument (Untuned)
3—5	Singing Tube Mirliton	2 Stones 2 Sticks 2 Strings Cuckoo-whistle 2 Tone Pipes	1 Stone 1 Stick 1 Tone-whistle 1 Tone-pipe Percussion Tube	Stone Stick Metal plate, tube Rattles: Straw, Wooden, Tin Hand Drums: Wooden box, Tin
5—10	Stone Play (8 tones) Xylophone (8 tones) Pan-pipe (5-8 tones) Bamboo-pipe	3-4 Stones 3-4 Sticks 3-4 Strings 3-4 Panpipe 3-4 Bamboo-pipe	1 Stone 1 Stick 1 Monochord 1 Tone-whistle 1 Tone-pipe Percussion Tube Double-whistle Double-pipe	Stone Stick Metal-plate, tube Rattles: Straw, Wooden, Tin

TOUR TO SCHOOLS IN SWEDEN

In May 1939, Paul Abbatt, B.A., will conduct a party of parents and teachers to visit schools and find out at first-hand about the educational system of that country. The tour will last 10-14 days, and fees will be kept as moderate as possible. Full prospectus from the Wayfarers' Travel Agency, 33, Gordon Square, London, W.C. 1.

Final page from 1938 catalogue *25 Best Toys for each age*, advertising music sessions with Ludwig Hirschfeld-Mack

Marjorie and Paul Abbatt with child in *All Purpose Trolley*, c.1969

ABBATT TOYS AFTER 1945

The survival of the Abbatt company through the Second World War must have required ingenuity and persistence, with materials and skilled workmen in scarce supply. However, in many ways the conditions for propagating their ideas as well as selling their products soon became far more favourable than they had been in the 1930s. At the start of the war, they gave up the workshop in Midford Place along with the flat in Tavistock Square, and used existing makers in High Wycombe, which was convenient for their country property at Ibstone in the Chiltern hills. Much later they moved their works to Stockport, Cheshire. This would have eased overheads, and many of their 1930s product lines stayed in the catalogue until the business was sold in 1973. Moira Keenan, who wrote on toys for the *Sunday Times*, reported reassuringly on their thirtieth anniversary in 1962 that 'their earliest designs are still their best sellers'.[101]

The 1950 catalogue shows many of the pre-war favourites, including Goldfinger's *First Train*, the *Funboat*, jigsaws and picture trays. This and the July 1949 catalogue (*Toys and Equipment for Schools and Nurseries*) both included the offer of small wooden items as 'Oddments for Free Play – a variety of turned wooden shapes and other oddments to be stimulating to free and imaginative play for little children. Collected as surplus to production in our factory, now offered at cost', plus a number of other 'surplus raw materials'. These were presumably the result of various wartime projects that had been suspended in peacetime.

Liner jigsaw, designer
unknown, from c.1950
(7 x 12 inches)

Ginger cat jigsaw,
designed by Jill Harrington,
from 1964
(9½ x 11½ inches)

Sailing Ship jigsaw,
designed by Janet Light,
from 1969
(7½ x 12 inches)

Dalmatian Dog jigsaw,
designed by Jill Harrington
or Freda Skinner, from 1964
(9½ x 11½ inches)

Newcomers whose names were now included in the catalogue with their products were Escor and Kiddicraft, both making wooden toys. Escor became a limited company on finishing military war work in 1948, and were finding a ready market for toys, although theirs were not cheap. Described as 'large, brightly painted wooden toys which screw together by means of large wooden nuts and bolts', Abbatts sold the '*Charabanc* with eight passengers', the *Fire Escape* (a ladder on wheels with four men) and *Tiplorry*.[102] These, together with bath toys in the form of boats, were all manned by Escor's smiling wooden figures with faces hand-painted on the rickety upper floor of their factory in a converted Methodist chapel in Christchurch, Hampshire, by a workshop team run by Ann Pitt who joined at 15 and stayed for 45 years doing the same job.[103]

Since both were founded in 1932, the Abbatts had been in friendly rivalry with Harry Page's Kiddicraft of Purley. Surviving a bankruptcy caused by over-buying before Christmas 1936, the firm began using injection-moulded plastics around the same time, since Page thought them more hygienic. Using the slogan 'Sensible toys', their products were often almost identical to Abbatts and appear to have been included but not credited in some pre-war catalogues. A later undated catalogue, apparently

Escor Toys, *Baby Car* and *Mini Racer*, from 1964

from the late 1950s, names them as suppliers of some of the early toys. Their plastic bricks were based on the principle later adopted by Gottfried Kirk Christensen for Lego in Denmark, and the cause of many years of litigation over the intellectual property of the concept. Page also wrote about toys in a way that corresponded closely with the Abbatts' outlook in *Playtime in the First Five Years*, issued first by a small publisher in Croydon in 1939, and then in a mainstream expanded edition in 1953 by George Allen and Unwin.

Multi-builder, produced by Nicol of Robertsbridge, East Sussex (launched just after the war and later incorporated in Gray-Nicholls sports equipment) was a kit of parts in beechwood adapted for making wheeled vehicles, promoted in post-war Abbatt catalogues. It was joined by *Connector*, a direct import from Denmark with the words 'Designed by Danish Architect Willy Fangel' prominently displayed on the packaging.[104] Composed of wooden rods, sawn like the pegs of the hammer pegs and pushed into cubes and discs to join them, *Connector* allowed for the rapid erection of frame-like shapes, including moving parts. Abbatts simply stuck their label on the lid of the wooden box, and this became one of their most enduring catalogue items.

Multi-builder by Nicol Ltd.
of Robertsbridge

Connector, designed by Willy Fangel

Diversions

Edward Newmark (1910-2004) has already come into this story. The Abbatts had met his wife, Gerda, in Vienna in 1931, and after she married Edward in 1937, they settled in Belsize Park in north London. After the war, they started Astu Ltd., making baby clothes and wooden toys, and then moved into importing toys from East Germay and Communist Eastern Europe, where Gerda's skills of language and negotiation were invaluable. In 1955, Edward became a junior partner in Abbatt and the manager of the shop. In that role, he became aware that Paul Abbatt's personal ambivalence about his role as a businessman inhibited the success of his company, explaining in an interview in 1981, 'his family had been a business family, and I think he had gone to university and hadn't gone into the business, and I think he had a bit of a block against being in business. He had developed the shop because it seemed the best way at that time'. Newmark concluded, 'like so many pioneers they started a bit too early, from the point of doing the right thing at the right time.'[105]

By the mid 1950s, however, the time was right. Individuals tended to have more disposable income and toy producers responded. Even allowing for inflation, the figure for production of games and toys in 1935 of £3.2m can be compared with £32.2m for 1955, and it then more than doubled over the ten following years.

Apart from a baby boom, there was the complete reconstruction of the educational system, involving new buildings and new pedagogy to go with them, thus ensuring sales to education authorities and individual schools. While in most European countries the age for starting school was six or seven, in Britain it was five, meaning that play was a much more significant part of the first years of education. Thus, as Edward Newmark explained in 1968, 'it is the infant school teachers who have created the demand for good toys in this country, and teachers see toys in a way parents never see them.'[106]

One consequence of Paul's disenchantment with commercial life was that in 1951 he and Marjorie established Children's Play Activities Ltd. (CPA), with Paul as Secretary and Marjorie as Treasurer. It was a not-for-profit body, endowed with shares in Paul and Marjorie Abbatt Ltd., and because it helped support the sales side, it was in fact a shrewd business move, while entirely in line with the philanthropic aims at the outset, which were the underlying motive. This will be discussed further in the next chapter, but the direct outcome was that the

Paul and Marjorie Abbatt,
Abbatt shop, Wimpole Street. 1963

shop seems to have taken a more independent course, compensating for his absence with some new approaches.

In the same period in the early 1950s, Marjorie became very involved not only in CPA but also in Artists for Peace (founded in 1950 By Ruskin Spear, Josef Herman and Carel Weight). She invited her niece, Felicity, who since childhood had found Paul and Marjorie more sympathetic than her own parents, to come and manage the shop.[107] Felicity recruited a group of female friends as staff and rejuvenated the approach to selling for a period of about five years before Marjorie returned. For someone of such generally liberal views, her attitude as a manager was surprisingly rigid in respect of allowing staff even minor flexibility in their working hours and other matters, so that Felicity soon resigned, while remaining a good friend of the couple, Paul in particular.

While Newmark was running the shop, he wanted to update the image of the business and was introduced to a young graphic designer, Ken Garland (b.1929), who was already working on *Design* magazine, published by the Design Council. A friend of the editor, Boris Ford, had recently been recruited for CPA, and through this connection, Garland was invited by Newmark to introduce a more up-to-date style in the Abbatt catalogues

and other printed material, but was not available for the longer term. As he has recounted, 'Edward Newmark let me know that he was becoming rather impatient with the Abbatts' regime, because he thought they were just sitting in their beautiful shop designed by Ernö Goldfinger in Wimpole Street and they didn't want to do very much. They just liked it the way it was. If one was cruel one might [say] this was their child whom they didn't want to grow up.'[108]

The result of this frustration was that in 1960, Newmark accepted an invitation from James Galt and Co. Ltd., based in Cheadle, Cheshire, where he transformed what for many years had been a trade supplier of school equipment into a retail and manufacturing business that soon overshadowed Abbatts. Rupert Webb (b.1928), architecture-trained son of the then-chairman of Galt who was related to the founding family, was responsible for this transformation, having joined the company in 1953. He went on to develop ten of their own shops, including a former tailor's shop at the north end of Carnaby Street, well-placed to capture the spirit of the

Catalogue page cover and letterhead
by Ken Garland, c. 1957-8

sand and water

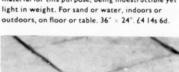

Paul and Marjorie Abbatt (World Export) Ltd   94 Wimpole St London W1   Telephone Langham 3884

ABBATT
TOYS

Water or sand tray. Made of fibreglass, an ideal material for this purpose, being indestructible yet light in weight. For sand or water, indoors or outdoors, on floor or table. 36″ × 24″. £4 14s 6d.

the right toy   for the right

Sandpit. The larger the sandpit the better, space or other factors permitting. A base is not necessary but if tiles are laid on the ground to help conserve the sand, they should be left loose to facilitate drainage. Constructed of very stout weather-roofed timber this Sandpit may be left permanently out of doors without attention. Delivered flat, easily screwed together, 6 sizes: ′ × 3′, £5 2s. 3′ × 4′, £5 12 6d. 4′ × 4′, £6 2s. 3′ × 6′, 6 12s 6d. 4′ × 6′, £7 2s. 6′ × 6′, £7 12s 6d.

Sandtools. Strong, plain beechwood; set consists f shovel, pounder, rake and hoe. 7s 6d.

Rubber bucket. Large, 3s 11d. Rubber spade and ake, 1s 3d each.

play
material
for
schools

Paul and Marjorie **ABBATT**

TOYSHOP

Creative Play catalogue, 1964. designer Donald Smith

1960s in this epicentre of pop fashion and conveniently close to London's biggest toyshop, Hamley's. Wimpole Street, although not more than ten minutes' walk away, probably had relatively little footfall from passing customers and as Paul Abbatt admitted,'We're slightly up-stage in Wimpole Street. One needs a little courage to enter such a shop.'[109] Because they already worked in wood for playground equipment, it went on to become Galt's defining material, as it had been for Abbatts from the start. They developed factories in Britain and others in Malta, Holland, Kenya, Ghana and the Ukraine, supplying not just their own retail customers but bigger players in the field such as Fisher Price.[110] In fact, in a *Listener* cartoon of October 1968, in his series satirising the trendy middle classes, 'Life and Times in NW1', Marc Boxer showed his anti-hero, Simon Stringalong, urging a mounted police officer and a TV news cameraman at the anti-Vietnam war demonstration in Grosvenor Square (notorious for the protestors hobbling the horses by rolling marbles on the roads), 'Can't you get a little nearer where the action is, officer? Don't worry about those marbles; they are probably only wooden ones from Galt or Paul and Marjorie Abbatt.'[111]

The Abbatts felt that Edward Newmark had taken with him most of their toy ideas, never protected as intellectual property. However, in a positive light, Galt understood the Abbatt mission and were able to push it far beyond its original limits, particularly by selling in their own shops outside London. Newmark left Garland the choice of whether to join him at Galt, and in 1961 he became their designer on a retainer. After Garland jumped ship, the Abbatts continued to commission their graphics in a similar style from Donald Smith (1927-2016), with Bauhaus-style lower case sans serif and bold colours with cut-out photographic images in uncrowded space. Around 1970, there was a further change of image with colour printing.

The Abbatt press coverage of the 1950s, in combination with the firm's own literature, helps to convey the accelerating public interest in toy design in the first 25 post-war years. Writing in *Design* in 1957, for example, the artist Roger Coleman noted the breathing space offered to British toy makers by the removal of German competition during and since the war, illustrating a combination of Abbatt toys with others from Kiddicraft, Chad Valley (the largest toy makers in Britain) and other much smaller concerns, all conforming to the same underlying message as the Abbatts'. Coleman condemned manufacturers and retailers for their 'toys which are far from sensible and leave a great deal to be desired in their workmanship ... a great many toys appear to exist in a kind of limbo of adult misconceptions, being neither suitable for the very young to exercise their manipulative talents, nor designed to meet the older child's demand for reality.'

Coleman was equally hostile to the 'design classic', Charles and Ray Eames' *House of Cards*, which he accused of having 'an adult's sophisticated recollection of childhood which is naturally lost on children'. He relished the vision of 'many enlightened parents who have stood by in uneasy silence while their children, with iconoclastic enthusiasm mutilated a *House of Cards*.'[112]

In 1963, the 27-year old Hunter Davies, standing in for Nicholas Tomalin at the Atticus column in the *Sunday Times*, made an entertaining overview of toy manufacturing, giving a view of the Abbatts as seen by a younger generation:

'At the peak of the posh end of the trade (they hate being called educationalists) are Paul and Marjorie Abbatt. For thirty years their toy shop, now in Wimpole Street, has been a stamping ground for all terribly sensible, terribly enlightened parents. … Mrs Abbatt is the business woman. She rarely suffers fools, but she has immense warmth and depth. … Mr Abbatt, who read mathematics at Cambridge, is fascinated by the theory of play and is prepared to spend

hours explaining to anyone the idea behind a toy.'[113] Amid other interesting personal details, the article describes how the couple were adapting to a world of plastic that still misunderstood the basics of good toys. 'Most Abbatt toys are made of wood. If people send them plastic stuff, they jump on it, and pull all the wheels. If it doesn't break, they might sell it.' An anecdote about one of their retail outlets conveyed the commercial problems caused by their high standards and prices, 'At one time they sold a lot of their toys to departmental stores, until one famous store sent them a curt memo. "Where you put in a screw, put in a nail. Where you put in a nail, put in glue."'

It was not all downhill, however, nor did the Abbatts stand still. New wooden items also began to appear in the catalogue such as 'Jumbling Jumbos', a set of coloured cut-out elephants whose legs and trunks interlocked so that they could be built up in different acrobat-like configurations. This was designed in 1955 by Isaac Weinfeld and Jan Vinot specifically for Abbatts.[114]

The 1962 catalogue showed Lego, marketed in Britain from 1959 onwards, described as 'the best made and most attractive of plastic constructional sets. Scope for simple little models, impressive buildings, even quite elaborate models.'[115]

Jumbling Jumbos, designed by
Isaac Weinfeld and Jan Vinot, 1955

In a very different spirit were Pollock's toy theatres, a post-war company founded to continue the Victorian business of Benjamin Pollock of Hoxton, which had in turn been rescued from receivership in the mid-1950s by the redoubtable Marguerite Fawdry, who established a shop and toy museum in Monmouth Street, Covent Garden.[116] Abbatts sold the superior *Regency* wooden theatre, with the play of *Aladdin* reproducing engravings based on actual stage settings of the 1840s, and a lighting set as an extra – one appears in the photograph of the Abbatts accompanying Hunter Davies's 1963 article, but after 1966, they seem to have been dropped from the range. The early 1960s catalogues also show miniature buildings in wood from Denmark and Germany as well as attractive *Harbour* and *English Village* sets made by Kiddicraft, in which a landscape setting could be created for the buildings.

Regency Theatre (first issued 1947 by Benjamin Pollock Ltd.), from 1962

New Toys: exhibition of British, Swiss and Scandinavian designers of international standing was an exhibition held over the midsummer weeks of 1963 at Wimpole Street, partly inspired by the designers whose work they had encountered through CPA. The invitation card described it as 'toys from the European Free Trade Association, [founded in 1960], and their own summer range of toys for out of doors.' Moira Keenan commented in the

Sunday Times that the predominantly wooden toys were 'beautifully displayed on open shelves', transforming the basement floor of the shop into 'an art gallery with as much appeal for adults as there is play value for children.'[117] This was the beginning of a new turn in making toys priced for and appealing to adults, not so much 'executive toys' as amusing items of interior décor. Several of the products and designers shown contributed to the stock in the following years.

Kiddicraft / Tiger Toys *English Village* 1959 onwards

105

Among the most enduringly famous of the ten exhibitors was Kay Bojesen (1886-1958), a Danish silversmith by training and author of the hanging wooden monkey, still a popular decorative item, and guardsmen, described by Keenan as 'the most "chocolate-cream" soldiers ever … 8 inches high in solid wood, with scarlet painted tunics and black bearskins'. Neither of these items joined the Abbatt range (no war related toys were allowed), but the rocking horse had appeared in the 1930s and *Family Out Driving* was added, along with the elaborate *Transport Set*, available in separate parts with road/rail ways and a car ferry with its own terminal.

The Swiss sculptor Antonio Vitali (1909-2008) began making toys during wartime military service, stimulated by wanting to give his young children something better than the standard commercial products. His simplified human and animal figures achieved international fame after the influential Swiss designer and teacher, Max Bill, promoted them in his 1952 book FORM, and they became part of the range of the American company, Creative Playthings, and also appeared in Abbatt catalogues as suitable for children. The 1964 catalogue included male and female figurines linked by a string, the *Pairli cradle toy*: To hang above the cot; to hold, wave about, bang together and bite. Beautiful polished

wood, sculpted.' There were teething toys, *Little Man* and *Duck*, the latter, 'a joy for mother and child, so elegant in shape. A little hand can hold or rock.'[118] There were items for an older child too, such as the *Sailing Boat*, *Engine*, and *Vitali train* with 'little removeable passengers' – this last featuring on the cover of the 1964 catalogue, in which the words 'Creative play' took precedence over 'Abbatt Toys'.[119] He explained his vision of toys in the words 'For children, toys must not be "toys" so much as "friends". Small children must be able to gain confidence from having them always at their side. This is what I keep in mind when I make toys.'[120]

The Swiss designer Kurt Naef (1926-2006) trained as a carpenter and began making and selling toys in 1956, later diversifying into reproductions of Bauhaus items. Definitely included in the Abbatt exhibition were his *Tawa* building blocks by the designer Christian Spiess, cut with facetted angles so that they form complex interlocking patterns. The 1964-5 Abbatt catalogue also included *Naef bricks*, a similar set cut from two inch cubes providing 'ingenious and surprising building and balancing possibilities.'[121]

P. Broste was a Danish manufacturer of sophisticated wooden animals and figures, working with the designer

play
baby

1. **Pairli cradle toy.** To hang above the cot; to hold, wave about, bang together and bite. Beautiful polished wood, sculpted. 5″ high. Designer Vitali. 3-15 months. 21s 11d, pack and post 1s.

2. **Shrimp Boat.** This is a solid little boat of shapely design with no bits or pieces to come adrift. 6″ long. Designers K. Notter and F. Hildred. 6 months-3½ years. 14s 11d, pack and post 1s 3d.

3. **Little Man teether.** 5½″ long, polished wood. Edges all rounded, nice to hold by head or tail, or bite. Designer Vitali. 3 months-1 year. 14s 11d, pack and post 9d.

4. **Duck teether.** 5½″ long. A joy for mother and child, so elegant in shape. A little hand can hold or rock. Designer Vitali. 3 months-1 year. 12s 11d, pack and post 9d.

5. **Tinkleblocks.** Polished wood; red, yellow and blue; a little bell visible inside. Shake and listen! 6-18 months. 3 in a set. 14s 11d, pack and post 1s.

6. **Wooden Rattle.** Smooth, light and strong. Unpainted beech. Designer Kay Bojesen. 3 months-1 year. 9s 11d, pack and post 9d.
   Teething Ring. Nice to grip, shake and bite. 3 months-1 year. 4s 11d, pack and post 9d.

Antonio Vitali wooden toys, 1964 catalogue

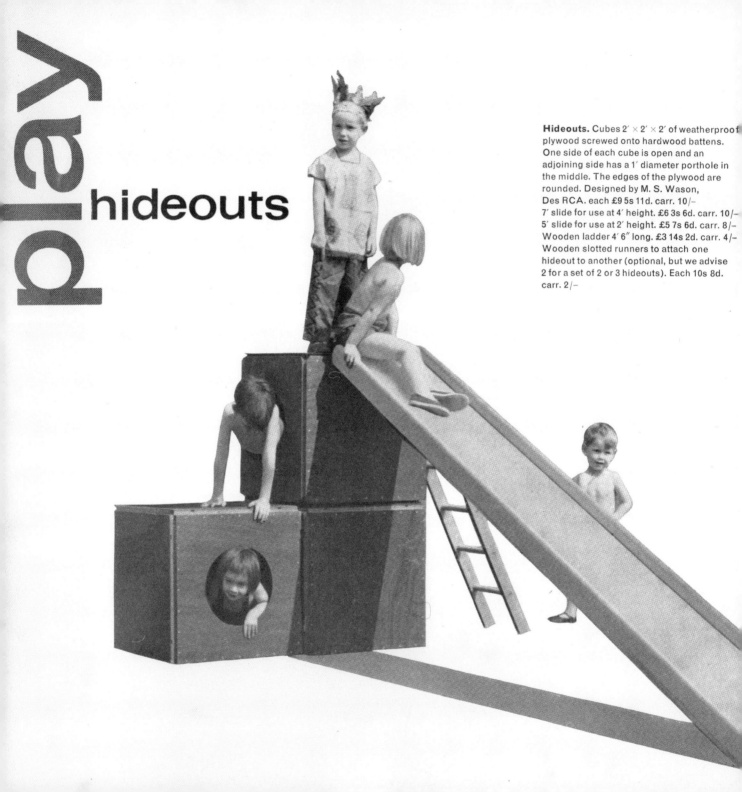

play
hideouts

Hideouts. Cubes 2' × 2' × 2' of weatherproof plywood screwed onto hardwood battens. One side of each cube is open and an adjoining side has a 1' diameter porthole in the middle. The edges of the plywood are rounded. Designed by M. S. Wason, Des RCA. each £9 5s 11d. carr. 10/-
7' slide for use at 4' height. £6 3s 6d. carr. 10/-
5' slide for use at 2' height. £5 7s 6d. carr. 8/-
Wooden ladder 4' 6" long. £3 14s 2d. carr. 4/-
Wooden slotted runners to attach one hideout to another (optional, but we advise 2 for a set of 2 or 3 hideouts). Each 10s 8d. carr. 2/-

J. Bentsen, and Kjeld Iversen, also Danish, chiefly known for a self-assembly plastic clock. Also represented were Community Playthings run by a Bruderhof community and still making wooden toys at Robertsbridge, East Sussex. The next name on the alphabetical list was Jill Harrington, who appears from 1964 onwards as the designer of *Baby Jigsaws* of steamroller, minicar, and other subjects, with no added detail on the plain coloured silhouette pieces. Audrey Stephenson (1929-1980), married to Donald Smith, was a designer and TV presenter on the subject of toys and therapy, whose *Beach* picture tray was incorporated along with the older designs by Freda Skinner and Madeleine Robinson. She also designed *House* and *Garden* insets where new pictures were revealed when the top pieces were lifted off.

From the Abbatts' viewpoint, however, the most enduring legacy of the show was their introduction to the English designer M. S. Wason, already the designer of a 'cot dangler'. His *Hideouts* were incorporated in Abbatts' catalogues from 1964 onwards, and given a spread to themselves. It could hardly have been simpler, consisting of cubes of waterproof plywood fixed on battens, with two foot sides, large enough to climb into through an open side, with a circular window/door on the facing side. Their versatility was emphasised in the catalogue entry,

'A number of hideouts side by side or on top of one another provide a warren or tunnel, as each has an open side and a port-hole in the adjoining side. Slides and ladders can be safely attached to the recesses or grooves on each edge. Thus children can clamber about both inside and outside the hideouts.' The scope was endless, including the potential for creating a shop, a post office or a puppet theatre, with sand-trays, water-troughs or slides hooked on as bridges between the cubes. 'The hideouts have all the requirements of good play material', the text concluded, 'strength, simplicity, adaptability, with both a play-interior and exterior, and within children's capacity to organise. They provide for both seclusion and sociability, imaginative and constructional play, and physical enjoyment.'[122]

Hideouts, designed by M. S. Wason for Abbatt, 1963

Hideouts on wheels, in a school playground, mid 1960s

Micki Leksaker railways from Gemla, Sweden (still in production) were also sold with an Abbatt label. Their magnetic couplings and jointed wooden tracks, first made in 1956, resemble the better-known Brio which followed a year later. Donald Smith's Garland-inspired catalogue style of 1962-66, with its spacious layouts and text pages on purple-tinted uncoated paper wrapping the glossy inner section of product photos and descriptions gave way by 1969 to a smaller format with colour pages included for the first time since a short-lived trial in the 1950s. The advisory text now runs alongside the images, still clearly in Paul Abbatt's voice, capturing the excitement of discovery and experiment at every stage of a child's development and quoting Susan Isaacs.

Micki Leksaker Railway,
first made 1956, sold by
Abbatt from c.1962

Opposite: Abbatt Toy Shop, Easter, 1962
Above: Abbatt Toys exhibition stand, 1962

Audrey Stephenson and Donald Smith met and were married in 1961, after his first wife, Jean, had died aged 32, leaving him with two small children. They formed a partnership, 'S & S Design', covering their work in graphics, toy design and displays, including window dressing for the Wimpole Street shop window during the 1960s, and special displays such as the one above, possibly made for a trade exhibition during the Abbatt thirtieth anniversary year.

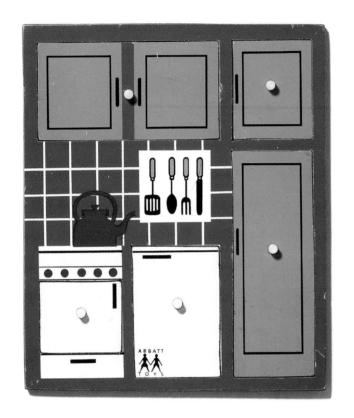 

Kitchen and *House*, Abbatt Inset Puzzles, designed by
Audrey Stephenson (11½ x 9 inches)

Before her death in 1980, Audrey was an Advisory member of the Toy Libraries Association, set up for the needs of children with disabilities, allowing their parents to bring home a variety of toys without the need to spend money. She was also an adviser on toys to the National Society for Mentally Handicapped Children, and helped the Design Council in toy selection. Audrey's designs for Abbatt include picture trays with images that are revealed when the pieces are lifted out. They offer a charming snapshot of their period in terms of the bright colours and the growing taste for stripped pine dressers, and kitchen implements hanging on the tiled wall.

it's time to play with Abbatt toys

Paul & Marjorie Abbatt toys
74 Wigmore St London W1

it's time to play with Abbatt toys, catalogue designed by Audrey Stephenson, 1973

The 1973 catalogue cover by Audrey reveals the move from 94 Wimpole Street to 74 Wigmore Street soon after the takeover by ESA. At this time, the logo was redesigned by Donald Smith, and Audrey edited the text from earlier writing by Paul Abbatt and her own contributions. In the same spirit of practical advice offered with insight and humour.

Another innovation was *Playplax*, the first product designed by Patrick Rylands in 1966, the chance result of his own thinking about play at the Royal College of Art, and his contact with Desmond Rawson of Hornsea Pottery in his home town of Hull, who put him in touch with a local manufacturer, Trendon.[123] Like Rylands' later designs for the Dutch company, Ambi Toys, it is exactly aligned with the Abbatt ideals of a toy that allows for many combinations and uses, while conveying bright colour and simple shapes, with its interlocking pieces.

The climbing frame text opens with a plaintive paragraph, 'The climbing frame replaces the vanishing trees, attics and barns, the ladders propped up against the hay, the wagon with a way of climbing up by the spokes of the wheel. It serves so many purposes of children that it may be said to validate and substantiate childhood and compensate it for what this century has lost of natural places to play.'[124] The

text for jigsaws contains both retrospect and an element of self-congratulation, as if Paul, who only had another two years to live, wanted to leave his record, 'Jigsaws for babies! Something unheard of years ago. From our beginnings, we have tried to supply playthings which would aid a child's development but which were not already available.'[125]

A new and rather different range of jigsaws now appears, under the title *Summer Days*, smaller than before at seven inches square, departing from the simple outlines towards more complex and crowded illustrations. There was another novelty, the larger *VC10* puzzle with a picture on each side of the pieces, showing a 'realistic' view of the British-made jet plane that flew from London to Montreal in 1964, together with an informative tableau of freight loading on the airport tarmac.

Dolls' houses had never been much of an Abbatt speciality, although when they appeared in the catalogue, they were appropriately modern in style. The 1969 catalogue shows a demountable product from Micki Leksaker in Sweden, with a chalet-style roof, strong wall colours and an appropriate range of furnishings.

Playplax, designed by
Patrick Rylands 1966,
sold by Abbatt from 1969

Dolls themselves were absent from all the pre-war catalogues, on the basis that other toy suppliers had the matter in hand. In 1969, however, *Sasha Dolls* made an appearance. 'The most life-like we have ever seen, beautifully modelled by Sasha Morgenthaler of Zürich. 16 inches high, soft but firm plastic. Limbs jointed, hair silky and washable; pretty and practical clothes to take off.' Boy versions were available as well.

Paul Abbatt died in June 1971, after a long illness. His *Times* obituary stated that 'today a clear sign of his influence is the fact that all over this country are shops that take toys seriously. To do so is no longer something peculiar to Paul and Marjorie Abbatt.'[126]

In 1973, Marjorie sold the business to the Educational Supply Association Ltd., a company producing equipment and stationary for schools, similar to Galts before they entered the retail field. She remained Vice-Chairman for a short period, but was drawn further into lecturing and working with the University of Nottingham.The Abbatt Toys brand survived into the early 1980s, although the shop did not last long after relocating to 74 Wigmore Street in 1973. The 1970s saw the beginning of a precipitous decline of the British toy-making industry, coming soon after its equally sudden rise in diversity and productivity.

However, this was not quite the end of the story. Abbatt's had a northern subsidiary in Stockport, Cheshire, which was sold separately by Marjorie to its manager, Terry Denton, and his Swedish wife, Gunvor, who had worked at the Wimpole Street shop. The business was renamed as ABCeta Playthings Ltd., and has continued into the present, now specialising in selling original *Sasha Dolls*, which were previously made in the Stockport factory.

Sasha Dolls, designed and made by Sasha Morgenthaler from 1963, sold by Abbatt from 1965. This image is from the 1969 catalogue

1936

1937

1938

1940

1969

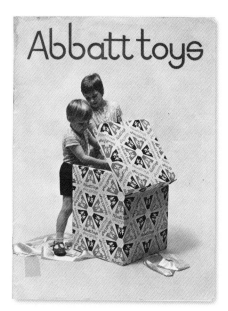

1970

1962

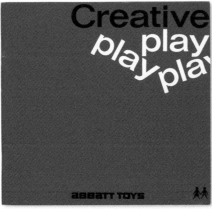

1963

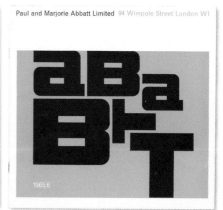

1965

1972

1974

1979

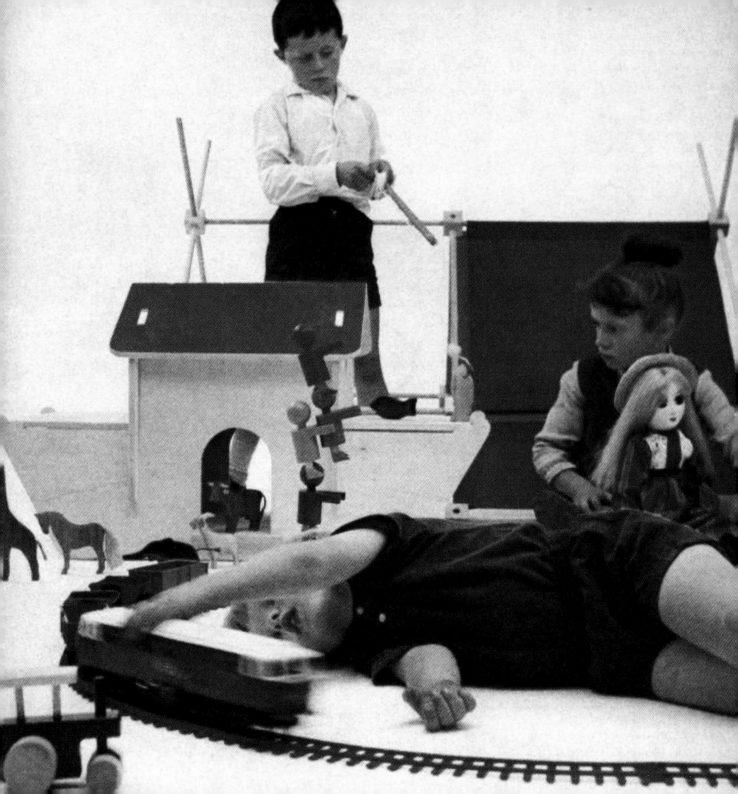

MODERN TOYS AND MODERN CHILDREN

Subtitling this book 'Modern Toys for Modern Children' tells only half the truth. Modernism is a recognisable construct in terms of art and design, and Abbatt products invariably conform to its best principles of clear form, honest and robust construction, and careful adaptation to 'function'. As a couple, they lived according to the same principles, with a sequence of austere flats in London and later in Brighton, sparsely furnished. Their choice of Goldfinger as their architect in the 1930s, rather than the more decorative Oliver Hill, affirmed their alignment with a sophisticated European stream of Modernism as much as their emulation of German or Austrian toys.

The real history of this movement does not begin where art historians place the beginning of modernism, around the turn of the nineteenth and twentieth centuries, but at least a hundred years before, in the book *Practical Education*, 1798, by Maria Edgeworth (1768-1849, better known as a novelist) and her father, Richard Lovell Edgeworth (1744-1817). It's opening chapter condemns elaborate and fragile toys that arose from what has been called 'the first consumer society', and takes seriously the child's needs on lines of tactile experience through re-enactments of grown-up life, art and craft, which barely differs from what the Abbatts proclaimed.[127]

Photo from *Design* magazine no. 227, November 1967. The original caption runs *'The Noah's Ark* by Geoffrey Baker for the Rumbold Gallery, is made from interslotting pieces of plywood; £8 5s 6d, from Hamley's. The German *Bau-bau* construction set makes up into a tent, house, etc. £9 19s 6d a box from Abbatt's. The *Big Big Train* by Triang, costs from £4 1s 6d. The Victorian doll costs £8 8s from Heal's. The steamroller is by Coach House Toys, from Habitat. The wooden animals are by Woodpecker Toys; and the plastic *Five Funny Men*, by Raphael Lipkin, cost 9s.'

While the Edgeworths' ideas did not sink entirely, the competition from the toy trade was a constant distraction. The tendency to sentimentalise children arising in the Edwardian years and persisting into the 1920s, with the cult known as 'the beautiful child', has been defined by Kimberley Reynolds as that 'childhood is characterised by its difference from maturity in being a uniquely "innocent" phase which must be preserved, prolonged and protected.'[128] This was reflected in toys and in the furnishing of children's domestic spaces with kitsch imagery in the interwar period, against which the Abbatts were reacting with their clear colours and almost bare walls. As Paul's introductory text for the Paris exhibition catalogue states of the items on show, 'in no respect is the construction weak or the design comic or sentimental.'[129] Whether the children received a positive benefit from this is impossible to prove, but for better or worse, they probably noticed the difference.

Another danger, in the Abbatts' view, was the over-didactic nature of many playthings arising out of educational theory, especially those of Froebel and Montessori that channelled children too tightly, suppressing their exploratory instincts. Their response was, in this context, remarkably sane.

The extent to which the Abbatts held the field of modern toys entirely on their own in the pre-war years has probably been exaggerated by the relative availability of information about them. However, in her book *Play and Toys in Nursery Years*,1938, Beatrix Tudor-Hart listed toys and equipment appropriate to the age of the child, and added a note listing three suppliers, Paul and Marjorie Abbatt, Educational Playthings Ltd. of 151 Haverstock Hill, Hampstead, and Kiddicraft. The first two are bracketed together as offering the most complete range of the best quality, but Educational Playthings, a company that has left no traceable mark in history, is noted as having 'a considerable selection at very moderate prices.'[130]

Subsequently, a different adult appropriation of childhood arose, based on the Modernism through which the Abbatts were trying to dispel the earlier one. When museums of art or design put on exhibitions about childhood, play or toys, they are apt to focus on the toys or toy-like objects produced by artists or other designers of note which are, in fact, of relatively little significance or value as toys for children, while leaving out much else that concerns that reality of children's play. It is an alternative easily-won appeal of cuteness not fundamentally different to the anthropomorphised animals of the past. A peak moment of this tendency came with the exhibition *Play Orbit* at the Welsh Eisteddfod and the Institute for Contemporary Art (ICA) in London in 1969, when artists and art school groups were invited to design toys or play environments, a fashionable trend of the time. One of the participants, Michael Pennie, was honest enough to admit, with regard to his 'Laddermax', that it was 'more significant to me as an artist than as a father.'[131]

The Abbatts, although welcoming more consciously 'artistic' toys into their shop and their catalogue through their 1963 exhibition, never fell too far into this trap, preserving their child-based ideas on which the firm was founded. But their effort was just as much to go back in time as to envisage a different world of the future, cleared as a blank slate. This was also consistent with the doctrines of Modernism, especially as these emerged in the 1930s with a less mechanistic and more sensuous approach to materials and techniques, exemplified in Le Corbusier's experiments after 1930 with rough stone masonry and coarse-grained timber as well as with concrete and steel. Paul's writings dwelt at length on ideas of how children must have learnt in pre-modern and pre-literate societies, informed by anthropology and popular ideas of childhood as a recapitulation of the developmental stages of human society.[132] These ideas were strongly influenced by the Order of Woodcraft Chivalry and its founder, Ernest Westlake, who used the phrase 'over-civilisation' to describe the problem of conventional schools and their learning methods.[133] In a lecture 'Woodcraft Training: The Basis of Technological Education', Paul Abbatt quoted his answer to a question about what buildings or equipment he would require for the education of a group of children. 'No buildings or equipment at all, just a stretch of woodland country with flowing water' was his reply.[134]

There was therefore a paradox at the heart of the Abbatt mission, because in the ideal condition of play there were no toys in the normal sense, although anything might be co-opted as play material. This did not deter them, because they rightly understood that 'over-civilisation' could not be reversed in a hurry and needed to be treated on its own terms, which implied both buildings and equipment, but with the difference that the underlying value of simplicity of objects and scope for improvisation in their use would be taken for granted. If there were to be toys, as Paul is quoted as saying, 'the best toy is the one made by father.'[135] Nonetheless, there are moments in the Abbatt catalogue when one feels they were selling items by way of apology for the fallen state of modern mankind, as seen in their 1969 catalogue text on the climbing-frame

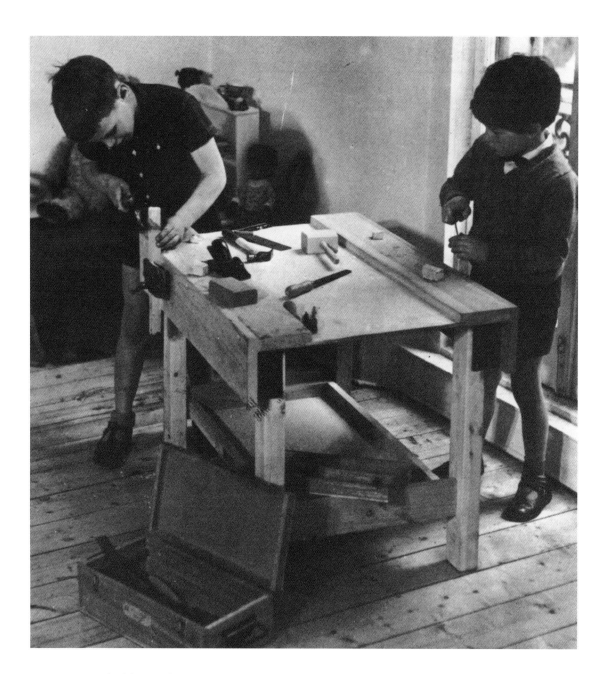

Carpenter's Bench, Abbatt catalogue 1969

as a poor substitute for tree climbing, quoted on page 116. Frequently, they emphasised that small children did not need a lot of toys. 'A child can be swamped by toys. Do not give too many. He will benefit from one toy rather than two at any one time, from a few more than from many. They are not trivialities', as Paul wrote in the brochure *Play & Toys* for Children's Play Activities in the early 1960s, now more comfortably changing his hat as a retailer for that of an educator.[136]

Another persistent theme in their products, unlikely to take its place in the history of toys as such, was the provision of tools and equipment, for carrying out household and garden tasks, and for art activities. The Abbatts were insistent that for children, play was work and vice-versa, and the handling of toys was a precursor to the use of real tools. In an early catalogue, the 'Toymaker Set' provided 'nailing board, hammer, nails and a plentiful supply of coloured wooden slats and discs.' With these, 'a boy or girl can quickly and easily make dolls' furniture, wagons, aeroplanes and all sorts of things.' The pieces could then be taken apart for a different project.[137] By 1936, the catalogue included a 'double carpenter's bench … enormously strong and solid.' While there was a tradition of woodworking in schools, this was a piece of real equipment with which real tools could be used, not

requiring a special woodworking room. One of these featured prominently in the Paris exhibition display in 1937.

Later, Paul wrote, 'to give a child carpentry tools implies some confidence in his ability to use them safely. Against the possible danger of scrapes and bruises has to be set his immense satisfaction in being the owner of a set of real tools. When we give him the tools we are giving him encouragement by showing our belief and confidence in him.'[138] These practical rather than fictional concerns, whether in a modern or historical setting, corresponded to a wider Modernist concern aimed less at a specific visual outcome, but concerned with excluding sentimentality of form and content as unworthy of the true nature of children.

These concerns were echoed in the Puffin Picture Book series conceived in practical production terms and edited by Noel Carrington who had shown his support for the Abbatts through publishing Paul Abbatt's articles in editions of *Design for To-day*, and was also the publisher, at Country Life, of Beatrix Tudor-Hart's 1938 book illustrating many Abbatt items in the hands of children, rather more effectively photographed in close-up than their own catalogue shots.[139] Initiated just before the

James Gardner, Puffin Picture Books, 1940-41

Puffin Books exhibition,
Abbatt shop, 1954

outbreak of war in 1939 and launched in December 1940, the Puffin Picture Books included some stories, but the emphasis was on factual information about everyday life, including making things.[140] There were several overlaps between this series and Abbatts, notably in the person of James Gardner, designer of the Abbatts' Zoo Zag and Airplane Snakes & Ladders in 1938 and author-illustrator of *How They Fly*, 1939, a history of aviation published by Carrington in his previous position at Country Life books. For Puffin Picture Books he produced *War in the Air*, 1940. Not surprisingly, the Abbatts were in touch with Carrington, and early in the war, Marjorie wrote to complain that he should not be using Penguin resources for producing books about war, but instead concentrating on peaceful subjects. Ernö Goldfinger also worked on one of several abortive Puffin Picture Books, with the title *Building a House*.

All these endeavours belonged in a period between the crystallisation of a broad ethos of Modernism that was largely adopted as a national style in the era of the post-1945 Welfare State, and the threat to its corruption that was perceived to come from the danger of television and comics, especially those imported from America, and the materialistic culture of consumerism that lay behind them. Writing in 1957, the year after independent television

began to broadcast, Paul saw toys as instruments in a bigger conflict. Teachers 'much wiser and bolder than parents in general', were 'conducting a kind of battle in the arena of the children's souls to help them keep alive their active appetite for the particularity of experience and to protect them against their vulnerability to the stereotyped and the passive. The teachers look for and find aids in anything the child can handle and work with pleasure – odd parcels of various timber, packing cases, even old motor cars and traction engines.'[141] What he described was, however, a close match to what children could see weekly after the launch of Blue Peter by the BBC in 1958, which convincingly held the field. Were the children watching imported American cartoons on ITV or those learning to make objects from scrap cardboard on Blue Peter the truly 'modern' ones? The likelihood is that if cultural pundits made an absolute distinction between these two offerings, the child audiences lapped up both equally.

In fact, both Paul and Marjorie made brief appearances on various BBC discussion programmes. In April 1939, Marjorie took part in 'From the Trees', on television, in which three attitudes to wood were discussed, the scientific, artistic and utilitarian.[142] With television becoming more mainstream, in 1960 Paul showed examples and talked about 'the right toy for the right age' for 'Family Affairs'. In a programme 'What next in toys?', he represented 'children' with the journalist Moira Keenan and John Heritage, followed with a section on 'adult' toys, that included a pioneer in this cross-over genre, the artist-toymaker Sam Smith (1908-83) together with crafts gallery owner, Henry Rothschild (1913-2009) and an unnamed 'consultant psychologist'.[143]

The history of educational toys still lacks a comprehensive overview such as would allow the Abbatts' contribution to be set alongside that of thinkers and producers in other countries. Amy F. Ogata's *Designing the Creative Child: playthings and places in mid-century America* does a thorough job in respect of the American post-war scene and its supporting ideologies, noting the urgency with which American parents turned to the idea of educational toys in the 1950s, making them part of a national movement. She writes, 'In my project, the nexus between scientific research on creativity, the consumption of toys and amusements in the name of raising "creative" children, and the official educational sphere of school building, art education, and the elevation of hands-on "discovery" in museums shows that the authentically creative individual self was internalised as the desirable goal, not only of post-war childhood but also of post-war adulthood.'[144]
There were unattractive aspects of didactic coercion in

this movement that hoped to improve the child's career prospects in science or technology by direct means.
A catalogue for the Playskool company, with an essay 'What Toys Shall I Buy for My Child?' by the Chicago child-development expert, Ethel Kawin, warned 'It is not enough that toys are educational – they must be correctly educational so that they teach the right things at the *right time* in the *right way*.'[145] It is unclear whether she would have applied this to an item picked out for mockery in the British press in 1950 as an example of 'a more progressive outlook on the American nursery front' : an advertisement reading, 'The Educational Toy Shop invites you to see now their toys of value for the Spring Time … Atomic Energy kit includes a Geiger counter that works. It does not make bombs … Psychologist in attendance.'[146]

Paul Abbatt's address to the Woodcraft Chivalry may have reflected this mood by emphasising play as a foundation for scientific discovery rather than as the key to child development or the working out of inner conflicts. Depending on the actual date of his words, this could have been a response to the nationwide anxiety generated by C. P. Snow's 1959 lecture, *The Two Cultures*, with its fear that British education and culture favoured the humanities at the expense of the sciences, and the imbalance needed to be redressed, combined with a background fear of Soviet ascendancy in space following the first Sputnik in 1957. Paul may also have been reflecting a type known in America as 'the savage boy inventor' – a 'presumed reader of handbooks and popular science manuals, derived from both manual competence and a streak of productive experimentalism.'[147]

Even so, the longer perspective of Abbatt texts and catalogues was consistent in its emphasis on a simple ideal of happiness through achievements both technical and emotional. While Paul Abbatt refined the specifics of 'the right toy for the right age' principle into a bar chart in the 1960s, he still made a wide range of allowance for different children's wishes and needs, also deflating scientific precision by explaining, 'Children will use them upside down and the opposite way from intended.'

Osbert Lancaster's 1950 cartoon (p.25) was not a lone voice of protest against parents who seemed to endanger their children by trying too hard and became caricatures of the over-earnest, but was mirrored on the other side of the Atlantic by a stream of visual jokes by Saul Steinberg. By 1962 however, there was already a reaction against 'everything being taken over by the press of practicality' when two researchers at the University of Chicago argued that the more decorated and representational but not

obviously useful 'floppy rag doll' or 'ancient lead soldier' might now be missing from the imaginative repertory of the child, unless they had been lucky enough to have a box of passed-down items from an older and possibly gentler world.[148] Something of this change seems to have occurred in England around the same time.

The photograph of Paul and Marjorie in their shop (p. 97) taken in 1963 for the *Sunday Times* showing crowded shelves behind them with a Pollock's toy theatre represented what Robert Louis Stevenson called 'art, folly or the bright eyes of children.'[149] Thus in toys as in parallel worlds of design, the constraints of Modernism began to be subverted by the hedonism of Post-Modernist plurality of modes of expression in what Roger Coleman in 1957 called 'make-believe' as opposed to 'practice play'. Arguably, the Abbatts remained more closely wedded to a prior model that best fitted a child's development up to the period known as 'latency', around the age of seven, rather than risking diluting their brand with too many of the brash and realistic products that had a stronger appeal beyond that age.

In 1982, the toy curator and historian Patrick Murray, noted that, in the light of a year in which toys derived from *Star Wars* were the best sellers, 'there is nothing new in this demand. What is new about realism in toys is adult squawking about it.'[150] If measured from Maria Edgeworth's 1798 book, the squawking, now approaching its bicentenary. was nothing new either. It will probably always be there.

Around 1967, the balance had been struck between over-seriousness and over-artiness, both of which conflicted with the reality of childhood. *Design* magazine emphasised the core of 'very capable, imaginative designers who design good, often exciting toys, which stand up to hard wear and which have been worked out with an understanding of a child's needs and problems.'[151] Having duly acknowledged the pioneering role of the Abbatts, the article went on to admit that 'words like *play value*, *a child's needs* and *educational* may sound heavy and humourless with overtones of the do-gooder about them. But one only has to go to a shop like Tridias in Bath, and look at the lively and colourful selection of glove puppets, jack-in-the-boxes, zithers (made especially for them), building sets, and a range of educational puzzles and geometric shapes more often seen in infant and junior schools, to realise just how wrong one can be.'[152]

Children's Play Activities

First suggested by Paul Abbatt in notes dating from 1947, and formally constituted in 1951, Children's Play Activities (CPA) aimed to 'extend the understanding of play as an element in mental and social education; to promote the design of good toys; to encourage safe and adequate provision for children's play; to provide a reference library of good play materials, equipment, books etc.'[153] A profile of the Abbatts in 1962 put it more succinctly 'set up … to study such problems as those of a child who lives on the twenty-ninth floor' (a problem that did not yet exist in 1951).[154] The charity was a limited company, holding 40% of the shares of the Abbatt company, and as the V&A description of their archive noted, 'in return for making CPA Ltd. more visible a door was opened for the Abbatts into academic circles and societies, which remained closed to other toy manufacturers.'[155] After what seems to have been a slow start, in 1956 CPA briefly employed Boris Ford as organising secretary, and during his seven months in the post, he convened two expert panels, one on the design of toys, the other on children's play, both reporting to the Council for Industrial Design. The enquiry provided scope for making international connections, with similar bodies in Germany and the USA. One of the main findings from the industry was the almost complete disregard of professional design. Instead, most manufacturing was 'a process of compromise, cost, plagiarism, or amateur suggestion.'[156] The report led to an exhibition at the Council's Design Centre in Haymarket, London, in September 1958.

One early if modest example of CPA activity in parallel with the business was a simple but attractive leaflet on *Toys for Sick Children*, 1957, with drawings initialed 'EP'. It was a decade or so before vaccinations for several infectious diseases became available, and it was normal for children to spend several weeks in bed before the age of ten. The leaflet spoke to parents in the same voice as the Abbatt catalogues, with a chart of appropriate toys, emphasizing the special value these could acquire at such times. It was picked up in an *Observer* article and no doubt elsewhere.[157] However, the aims of the charity were broad and at times Paul's dreams, including 'an advisory centre on play, play materials, and especially play space in an urban society where land has become too profitable to be used for playgrounds', failed to reach fruition.[158]

The journalist Betty Jerman who interviewed Paul was polite, but wrote in respect of long reports issued by the International Council for Children's Play, founded in 1959 by the Abbatts with German, Swiss and French sections, 'they are most interesting but left me thinking, "so what?"'.[159] It appeared that CPA had little contact with the Adventure Playground movement that was active in finding temporary play sites where they were needed. [160] It nonetheless undertook a survey of children's activities in their leisure hours. No questionnaire was drawn up and the range of topics was broad. Jerman reported the following year on the contribution of 'a class of boys between 10 and 11 in Northumberland' who 'sent vivid descriptions of self-invented games, adventures and activities.' Strikingly, however, none of their camps up trees or in caves involved places specially set up for children's play.[161]

The International Council for Children's Play (ICCP), still in existence, came into being at a conference at Ulm in Germany in 1959 at which 12 countries were represented. For the Abbatts, it may have seemed like a reprise of their honeymoon, but now in a Europe that instead of being threatened by political extremism was rebuilding from the ruins, even if fearful of the pace of modernization. The following year 50 representatives came to a conference at Brighton, organized by CPA, including some from Africa and India. A leading figure was the Austrian, Hildegard Hetzer (1899-1991), Paul and Marjorie's contemporary in age and a significant figure in the study of child poverty and play since the 1930s. It was probably from her that Paul took the phrase 'the right toy for the right age', and Jude Welton suggests that her search for 'a child's "organic relationship" with their world, however compromised by urban conditions, reflected his own grounding in the Order of Woodcraft Chivalry.[162] Early on, ICCP created a seal for certification of toys and in 1963 published *Gutes Spielzeug*, elegantly designed by the Hochschule für Gestaltung at Ulm, considered to be the successor to the Bauhaus. It was in fact a reprint of a 1954 touring exhibition catalogue, from which it seems likely that Paul Abbatt took the idea of bar charts showing the age range of different toys.[163] Following the Brighton conference, CPA published *A First Survey of Research on the Play of Children Below the Age of Nine* Years by U M Gallusser of UNESCO. At the conference in 1968, Marjorie was elected president.

In 1981, CPA was transformed into a grant-giving Children's Play Activities Trust Fund, based in the Child Development Research Unit at the University of Nottingham. It supported 'important films on play' and 'setting up a second research observation playroom in the University'.[164] After Paul's death in 1971, Marjorie continued the work with the fund, travelling to Nottingham, and Elizabeth Newson, wife and colleague of John Newson, recalled her as 'this tall, handsome woman who at 70 was still the epitome of elegance with her beautifully styled hair and Hardy Amies suit.' In later years, Marjorie remained active in the Trust, and 'despite her failing sight, her eyes would shine at some particularly happy scheme; whether making a teaching video on musical interaction therapy for autistic children (which went all round the world), setting up a playscheme for blind children, buying special equipment to allow a child with fragile skin to achieve play, or just taking children to the pantomime.'[165]

After she died and Elizabeth Newson's words were published in her *Guardian* obituary, Jack and Elizabeth Hubbard wrote an extended supplementary piece, describing how both Paul and Marjorie had helped them when they set up a community play centre in Brighton (where the Abbatts had a weekend flat), 'One highlight was an exhibition of toys and play materials supplied by various firms. At the centre stood not only Abbatt Toys, but Paul and Marjorie, talking with parents for most of the day. In the evening they gave a joint discourse on toys, toy-making and manufacture. Their knowledge and experience belied the quiet style with a skein of gentle humour. Childless, they understood children, families and play.'[166]

On this last point, Felicity Jaffé, Marjorie's niece, explains that Marjorie suffered a miscarriage that made it impossible for her to have children. As well as putting her and Paul's energy into the business and its wider mission through Children's Play Activities, at an earlier point she and Paul had made a successful effort to help a family escape the Nazis and find a place in England. Milan Morgenstern, mentioned on p.10, had been a student at the Bauhaus in the Weimar period before 1923, one of many Viennese students who joined the school to follow the master Johannes Itten, and subsequently headed a counselling service for juvenile lawbreakers in Berlin. He visited London shortly after the family had left Berlin for the temporary safety of Vienna in 1933, and Paul urged him not to return, but he insisted on remaining with his family. Following the arrival of the Nazis in 1938, however, his wife Sophie (née Hirschberg, an educator of disabled children) who spoke English better, wrote to ask for help, and received a letter from Paul, who like Marjorie spoke German well, deliberately dated from before the Anschluss.

Having met the parents and their two children, Eva (1926-1998) and Franz (d.2001), from the boat at Folkestone and helped them through Immigration, they reached London and were offered the Abbatts' Tavistock Square flat. Sophie recalled in an interview in 1981, 'There stood Marjorie, before the door, and had her suitcases in her hand … and said "Oh, we love it so very much to be in a hotel"', meaning that they were moving out temporarily to leave their guests to settle in. 'It was all full with flowers, everything for the children was there.'[167] Eva recalled, 'sliding into their drawing room with a floor as smooth as a skating rink'.[168] She was found a place in the Quaker school at Croydon and went on to St Anne's College, Oxford. Franz, who took over his father's work in education, attended Burgess Hill School, paid for by Paul, who took an active interest in his progress. Sophie recalled their first Christmas with the Abbatts at in their cottage reached through snowy woods at Ibstone. 'There was a huge fireplace, and enormous blocks of wood. And you could sit in the fireplace – it was wonderful. And snowing – the woods. And we had snowball fights of course – because they both were wonderful with the children. I always wanted them to have children. They were so wonderful with children.'[169]

Milan, already an expert in the study of toys for disabled children, was initially interned but was able to resume his work on toys, and to prepare an English language version of his book on Special Education (with Helen Low Beer), originally published in Leipzig in 1936 as *Heilpädagogische Praxis*.

Practical Training for the Severely Handicapped Child, by Milan Morgenstern, Helen Low-Beer and Franz Morgenstern, Heinemann 1966

Milan died in 1954, his work was carried on by Franz, who later became a child psychiatrist at the University of London Institute of Education and author of standard textbooks, and was listed as co-author of *Practical Training for the Severely Handicapped Child*, 1966.

Two years later, *Abbatt Developmental Toys for Assessment and Training*'were included in the Abbatt catalogues and promoted as equally suitable for small children of any kind. *Threading Toys*, designed by Milan Morgenstern, were a range of three differently shaped wires with a wooden ball at the end for protection, and a series of coloured wooden rings to snake around the right angles or spiral. As the catalogue suggested, 'these toys have the fascination of puzzles and help develop manipulative skill of wrist and arm.'[170]

The Times reported on the launch of this range in August 1968, including 'winding boards' to 'help the child coordinate hand movements into different rhythms', and 'a mosaic floor composed of inter-relating geometric shapes in vivid colours – giant stars, octagons and triangles – designed to encourage handicapped children to play together.'[171] With Franz's involvement as translator, the Abbatts continued to promote the work of Milan with the development of toys for disabled children using funding from CPA. Marjorie reported how the toys were 'pounced on' at the Hannover toy fair, while the ICCP proposed a central lending library for such toys in each country. As Betty Jerman commented, 'the principle of the toy being part of the development of a child, which the Abbatts have so strongly advocated, is seen here in its essence.'[172] Eva, who became an East German citizen with her husband Josef Brück and worked as a translator, was still in communication with Marjorie following the fall of the Berlin Wall in 1990, with forebodings for the future.

Eva's fond recollections of the couple make an appropriate note on which to finish. 'Paul and Marjorie belong to those who will not only stay alive, but they will stay young, always: Marjorie with her lovely gentle blue eyes, light hair and expressive face, so pleasant to hear speaking, generous, straightforward, full of humour and many-sided interest; a personality no one could remain indifferent about with a great "power of radiation", unusual intelligence and the ability to solve complicated problems with virtuosic simplicity. Paul – outwardly reserved, a very calm, balanced personality of great will power, but to all those who knew him more closely, a man of warmth, humour, generosity – and fine sensitivity and tact. …

'I could never say where Paul began and Marjorie ended – or vice versa. There are rare examples – particularly in the complicated, conflict-ridden world of today – of two people better matched or closely melted into one: in personal life and the hard matter-of-fact world of profession and business. … the charming and competent way in which both dealt with their staff and customers at the shop and the great taste and creativeness in their so human business for the benefit of growing children. …and many people whose lives they saved and whom they helped with great generosity and utter selflessness, never making the others feel humiliated in any way, with natural grace and warm friendliness, never once asking for anything in return.'[173]

NOTES

INTRODUCTION

1   Ben Duncan, 'Profile: Marjorie Abbatt – toy maker extraordinary', *Times Educational Supplement*, 1 June, 1973, p.10

2   Ibid.

3   Elizabeth Newson, 'Marjorie Abbatt', *Guardian*, 19 November 1991, quoting from MA's account given to Jude Welton.

4   Jude Welton, *Paul and Marjorie Abbatt: The Story and Ideas behind Abbatt Toys*, MA Thesis, University of Nottingham, Child Development Research Unit, 1980, p.10

5   Paul Abbatt, "Toys and Play", *Education* (Department of Education, New Zealand), vol.6, no.2, June 1957, p.30

6   Welton, 1980, p.17

7   See Carolyn Steedman, *Childhood, Culture and Class in Britain*: Margaret McMillan, 1860-1931 (New Brunswick, Rutgers University, 1990)

8   On Wilson, see Siân Lliwen Roberts, *Place, Life Histories and the Politics of Relief: Episodes in the life of Francesca Wilson, Humanitarian Educator Activist*, PhD, University of Birmingham, 2010 (https://etheses.bham.ac.uk/id/eprint/848/1/Roberts10PhD_A1a.pdf). Quote from p.52.

9   See D. E. M. Gardner, *Susan Isaacs, the first biography* (London: Methuen Educational, 1969)

10 Welton, 1980, p.23

11 'Idealists in the Toyshop', *Observer*, 2 December, 1962, p.13

1. ABBATTS IN BLOOMSBURY

12 'Tour of the Shops', *Observer*, 19 December 1934, p.28

13 '30 years' in *Paul and Marjorie Abbatt Toys*, catalogue 1963-64, p.xiv

14 Paul Abbatt, *Education*, op.cit. p.30

15 No copy of this catalogue has come to hand as yet.

16 Owing to changes in national formations and boundaries during his lifetime, Goldfinger's nationality is difficult to state briefly. Of Jewish family, he was born as a citizen of the Austro-Hungarian Empire, in part of Transylvania that was allocated to the newly-created state of Romania in 1919. However, during the Second World War his nationality was officially Polish. He became a naturalised British citizen in 1947

17 Goldfinger to Paul Abbatt 6 March, 1935. Ernö Goldfinger Papers, RIBA Archive, Box 65. In a letter of 12 March to Lubetkin, Goldfinger describes the Abbatts thus: 'c'est des gens charmants, de grands amis de moi'.

18 On Pomona Toys, see https://www.dollshousespastandpresent.com/issue7nov2010p5.htm; Mary Horder was aged 22, and continued making toys after the war in partnership

    with Maita Frank, see https://www.vam.ac.uk/moc/wp-content/uploads/2016/03/FRAN-Catalogue-18.02.15_4b376ddc1424c384a7f0b2da565e278c.pdf

19 *Edinburgh Evening News*, 21 June 1933, cutting in Oliver Hill's scrapbook, RIBA Archives, London.

20 Paul Abbatt, 'The Child's World: Psychology in Toys and Games', *Design for To-day*, No.8, December 1933, 290-297.

21 See Lisa Sheridan, *From Cabbages to Kings* (London, Odhams Press, 1955)

22 *Exhibition of Contemporary Industrial Design in the Home, Dorland Hall, 18, Regent Street, SW1*, 1934, p.75. An axonometric drawing of the stand is in the RIBA Drawings Collection and reproduced in Robert Elwall, Ernö Goldfinger (London, Academy Editions, 1996), p.43. The display does not match the catalogue text.

23 Ibid.

24 Ernö Goldfinger Papers, RIBA Archive, Box 65

25 H. Pearl Adams, 'Woman and her World: The last-minute present', *Observer*, 23 December, 1934, p.15

26 H. Pearl Adams, 'Woman and her World: The children's year', *Observer*, 6 June, 1935, p.28

27 Welton, 1980, p.60

28 Edward Newmark, 'British Toys', *Journal of the Royal Society of Arts*, January 1968, p.142

29 Paul and Marjorie Abbatt Ltd., *Games and Toys*, April 1935, p.56

30 'A Child's Choice' advertisement, *Nursery World*, 4 December 1935, p.47

31 Ibid.

32 Abbatt advertisement, *Games and Toys*, February 1935, p.179

33 Kiddicraft Hammerpeg advert, *Nursery World*, 4 December 1935, p.119

34 Adverts and editorial in *Nursery World*, 4 December 1935 and 1 July 1936.

35 https://www.early-education.org.uk/extended-history-early-education

36 Board of Education, Report of the Consultative Committee on Infant and Nursery Schools, 1933, p.41

37 H. Myles Wright and R. Gardner-Medwin, *The Design of Nursery and Elementary Schools*, London, Architectural Press, 1938, p.15, cited in Elizabeth Darling, *Re-Forming Britain* (Abingdon, Routledge, 2007), p.97

38 'The Nursery School … A New Association Formed', *Manchester Guardian*, 26 June, 1923, p.11

39 'Nursery Topics of the Week' by the Editor, *Nursery World*, 22 January, p.281 and 5 February, 1936, p.345

40 Paul Abbatt to Ernö Goldfinger, 20 April 1934. Ernö Goldfinger Papers, RIBA Archive, Box 65

2. GOLDFINGER AND ABBATT

41 Goldfinger to Paul Abbatt, 9 November 1933. Ernö Goldfinger papers, RIBA Archive, Box 65.

42 Paul and Marjorie Abbatt, *25 Best Toys for Each Age*, 1938, p.21

43 A few examples of this chair were made following the original drawings by Chris McCourt of Isokon Plus Ltd. in 1996 for display by the National Trust at 2 Willow Road. No original examples have been traced. The request for a price quote from Aircraft Ltd. is in a letter of Goldfinger's to Marjorie Abbatt of 5 June 1937. The prices ranged from ten to thirteen shillings according to the height of the chair, which Goldfinger declared 'very high'. They must either have beaten the price down or gone elsewhere, because the retail price in the catalogue was 10/6 for 10 inches high, and 11/6 for 12 inches high.

44 B. M. Ahlberg, 'Britain in Foreign Eyes', *Daily Telegraph*, 21 August, 1937.

45 Gavin Stamp, 'Conversation with Ernö Goldfinger', *Thirties Society Journal*, no.2, 1982, p.21

46 Abbatt catalogue, *Educational Toys*, 1936.

47 Among other manufacturers listed in the catalogue are Britains, Meccano, The Guild of Treasure Seekers, Pomona Toys and Jungle Toys.

48 See https://www.simonwilley.com/easiworkltd

49 Paul Abbatt, 'The Child', *Guide to the exhibits in the Pavilion of the United Kingdom, International Exhibition, Paris, 1937*, London: HMSO, 1937, p.236

50 See Duncan Forbes, ed., *Edith Tudor-Hart: in the shadow of tyranny*, Ostfildern: Hatje Cantz, 2013 and the film, *Tracking Edith* (2016), written and directed by Peter Stephan Jungk. Edith Tudor-Hart's sister-in-law, Beatrice Tudor Hart, ran the Fortis Green Nursery School in London where Abbatt toys and equipment were used.

51 Goldfinger to Sage & Co., Gray's Inn Road, 13 July 1937. Goldfinger papers, RIBA.

52 'The MARS Group exhibition of the elements of modern architecture', *Architectural Review*, March 1938, p.114

53 See Andrew Saint, general editor and Peter Guillery and Colin Thom, editors, *Survey of London volume 51: South-East Marylebone*, New Haven and London, Yale University Press, 2017, pp.255; 263-4; 356-7.

54 'Current Architecture 2', *Architectural Review* January 1937, pp.24-25

55 Fiona MacCarthy, 'Design in October: Playshops', *Guardian* 17 October 1967, p.6

3. THE ABBATT TOY RANGE BEFORE 1939

56 Edward Newmark, Interview 28 January 1981. Manuscript in possession of Felicity Jaffé. Interviewer's name not given.

57 The specific credits to Paul Abbatt are No.174 Cone Colour Cart; No.176 Hammernail alphabet; No.180 Rattle String and No.181, Baby Rattle.

58 Anita Christopheren, 'Toys to attract the …', unidentified newspaper cutting, 6 October 1962

59 Undated catalogue, pre-1936, with cover drawing by Madeleine Robinson, in V&A Museum of Childhood Abbatt Archive ('Robinson' hereafter), unnumbered pages.

60 Undated catalogue, pre-1936, in landscape format ('Landscape' hereafter), p.3. The date may be determined by the appearance in it of two small girls as models who also appear on the cover of *Design for To-day*, December 1934.

61 Two copies of *25 Best Toys* have been used for this research. One with a red cover appears to date from 1937 (the publication year of the last in a series of pamphlets 'Concerning Children' edited by Susan Isaacs for the University of London Institute of Education and the Home and School Council. The version with the same cover design in pale blue is datable to late 1938, since it carries a notice for a guided tour of Swedish schools in May 1939.

62 'The Happy Nursery', *The Lady*, 3 August, 1939, p.139

63 Welton, 1980, p.32

64 'Gift Ideas for Everyone', *The Lady*, 30 November 1939, p.693

65 *Educational Toys* catalogue, c.1936

66 The authorship is given in the catalogue of *Britain Can Make It*, 1946, item 173, p.105

67 'Robinson' catalogue

68 'Landscape' catalogue, p.8

69 Susan Isaacs, *Intellectual Growth in Young Children* (London: Routledge & Sons, 1930), p.268

70 *Educational Toys* catalogue, from 29 Tavistock Square, datable to 1933-34.

71 Abbatt Toys catalogue, 1970, pp.17-18

72 'Robinson' catalogue, page 8.

73 *Army & Navy Stores Ltd., General Price List 1935-36*, p.909. The Abbatt 'Peg and Block Trolley' appears on the same page.

74 Illustrated in *The Lady*, 30 November, 1939, p.693

75 *Toys and Books for Young Children* catalogue, 1950.

76 Wikipedia 'Jungle gym', accessed 9 August 2020. Hinton's father, Charles Howard Hinton, an English mathematician and explorer of the fourth dimension had built a similar frame for his son to learn spatial coordinates.

77 Susan Isaacs, *The Nursery Years* (London: Routledge & Kegan Paul, 1929), pp.125-6

78 This clip is included in the introductory film for visitors to No.2 Willow Road, Hampstead (National Trust)

79 *25 Best Toys for each age*, 1938 catalogue.

80 Ibid.

81 Isaacs 1929, p.127

82 Welton, 1980, p.41

83 Atticus (Hunter Davies), 'An ostrobogulous year for the toy men', *Sunday Times*, 29 December, 1963, p. 19

84 1938 catalogue p.35

85 'Robinson' catalogue.

86 Reproduced in Alan Powers, *Modern: The Modern Movement in England* (London: Merrell, 2005), p.38

87 *25 Best Toys for each age*, 1938 catalogue.

88 Sheila Mitchell, Obituary of Freda Skinner, *Independent*, 30 July 1993.

89 Welton, 1980, p.38

90 Welton, 1980 p.36

91 See https://britishtoymaking.wordpress.com/2012/08/02/conserving-the-british-toy-making-archive/ (accessed 16 August 2020)

92 Anita Christopheren, 'Toys to attract the …', unidentified newspaper cutting, 6 October 1962

93 *Educational Toys* catalogue

94 1938 catalogue p.31

95 The item is commonly dated to 1951, but it appears in the 1938 catalogue. Gardner's memoirs, *Elephants in the Attic*, (London, Orbis, 1983) do not mention the Abbatts.

96 Edward Bawden made a picture map for a London Zoo Guide with some similarities, although the animals themselves are not depicted.

97 1938 catalogue

98 The later history of Escor is colourfully recounted at https://www.vam.ac.uk/moc/wp-content/uploads/2016/03/MOC-BTMOH-39-04-Peter-Thorne-FINALISED-Transcript_6837b6cd0739229be59df36e3ff2f2f8.pdf

99 1938 Catalogue p.48

100 Paul and Marjorie Abbatt to L. Hirschfeld-Mack, 5 December 1938. University of Melbourne Archives 1971.0009.00048.

4. ABBATT TOYS AFTER 1945

101 Moira Keenan, 'Toys to stand the test of time', *Sunday Times*, 7 October, 1962, p.38

102 Abbatt *Toys and Books for Young Children*, July 1950

103 Museum of Childhood, British Toy Making Project, interview with Mr Peter Thorne, 2012, p.16 (as note 98)

104 The first datable appearance in an Abbatt catalogue appears to be c.1964. Willy Fangel seems to have left few traces in his role as an architect.

105 Edward Newmark, interviewer unknown, 28 January 1981. Felicity Jaffé archive.

106 Edward Newmark, 'British Toys', *Journal of the Royal Society of Arts*, January 1968, p.150

107 Welton, 1980, p.105. Marjorie Abbatt was on the selection panel for Artists for Peace exhibition in 1953 – information courtesy Tanya Harrod.

108 https://www.vam.ac.uk/moc/wp-content/uploads/2016/03/MOC-BTMOH-14-04-Ken-Garland-FINALISED-Transcript_9a49582eb1478d4f98440182d0c9efbd.pdf, p.6

109 'Idealists in the Toyshop', *Guardian*, 2 December 1962 p.13

110 Information from Museum of Childhood, British Toy Making Project, Interview with

Rupert Webb, 2012, Galt Rupert-Webb-FINALISED-Transcript_78dda2d1764fa1a9735b3c5cac938332

111 Marc Boxer, 'Life and Times in NW1: Where the action is', *Listener*, 31 October 1968, p.16

112 Roger Coleman, 'Toys: manipulation and make-believe', *Design*, no 108, 1957. p.31

113 Atticus (Hunter Davies), 'An ostrobogulous year for the toy men', *Sunday Times*, 29 December, 1963, p. 19

114 https://www.planetutopia.co.uk/listing/565669953/jumbling-jumbo-stacking-elephant-toy

115 Abbatt Toys, 1962-63, p.29

116 See Alan Powers, 'The Toy Theater ; Revival and Survival of an English Tradition' In David Buckingham and Jeffrey Goldstein, eds., *Toys, Games and Media* (Mahwah, New Jersey, Lawrence Erlbaum, 2004), pp. 11-18

117 Moira Keenan, 'Free Trade in Toys', *Sunday Times*, 23 June, 1963, p.34

118 *Creative Play 1964-65* catalogue, p.1

119 Ibid., p.10

120 Translation via Japanese, from *EDU-TOY, edutainment toy series vol.1 wood: EDU-TOY NAEF and European wooden toys*, kindly contributed by Everina Loane.

121 *Creative Play 1964-65*, catalogue, p.25

122 *Creative Play 1964-65*, catalogue, unnumbered page 'Hideouts'.

123 https://www.theguardian.com/lifeandstyle/2014/jun/25/patrick-rylands-toy-design-playplax-bird-fish-bath-duck

124 1969-70 catalogue, p.9

125 Ibid., p.20

126 'Mr Paul Abbatt, Co-founder of a famous toyshop', *The Times*, 16 June 1971, p.16

5. MODERN TOYS AND MODERN CHILDREN

127 Neil McKendrick, John Brewer and J. H. Plumb, *The Birth of a Consumer Society: the commercialism of eighteenth century England*, (London: Europa, 1982). *Practical Education* is available on https://archive.org/details/practicaleducati00edge

128 Kimberley Reynolds, *Children's Literature in the 1890s and the 1990s*, (Plymouth: Northcote House, 1994), p.4

129 Paul Abbatt, 'The Child', in *Guide to the Exhibits in the Pavilion of the United Kingdom, International Exhibition, Paris 1937*, (London: HMSO, 1937), p.236

130 Beatrix Tudor-Hart, *Play and Toys in Nursery Years* (London: Country Life, 1938), p.81

131 Jascia Reichardt, ed., *Play Orbit*, (London & New York, Studio International, 1969), p.137

132 Although reflected in the lengthier texts in Abbatt catalogues, Paul Abbatt's more substantial writings take the form of typescript and manuscript drafts and lecture scripts, chiefly in the Archives of the V&A Museum of Childhood, Bethnal Green. Jude Welton (op.cit) transcribes the complete text of a lecture 'Woodcraft Training: The Basis of Technological Education', pp.115-143, no date given.

133 Ernest Westlake, cited in Derek Edgell, *The Order of Woodcraft Chivalry, 1916-1949, as a New Age alternative to the Boy Scouts* (Lewiston New York; Lampeter, E. Mellen Press, 1992), p.87

134 Welton, 1980, p.142.

135 Betty Jerman, 'Toys for Development', *Guardian*, 9 October 1968, p.9

136 *Play & Toys*, (London: Children's Play Activities Ltd.), undated, facing p.1

137 'Landscape' catalogue, p.3

138 *Play & Toys*, p.21

139 The photograph's in Beatrix Tudor-Hart's book were by Ergy Landau (1896-1967).

140 See Joe Pearson, *Drawn Direct to the Plate, Noel Carrington and Puffin Picture Books*, (Penguin Collectors Society, 2010)

141 Paul Abbatt, 'Toys and Play' in *Education* (Wellington, New Zealand), vol., no.2, June 1957, p.32

142 18 April, 1939, 'From the Trees', with Mary Field, Polly Hall Clarke and Marjorie Abbatt.

143 'Family Affairs, Living through Playing', 25 February 1960; 'What next in toys?'. On radio, Marjorie appeared in overseas programmes 'Mainly for Women' 1948 and 'Looking at Britain', 1949, and Paul on 'Woman's Hour', 1958 and 'Parents and Children', 1963. Information courtesy Jeff Walden, BBC Written Archive.

144 Amy F. Ogata, *Designing the Creative Child: playthings and places in mid-century America*, (Minneaoolis, University of Minnesota Press, 2013), p.xxii

145 Amy F. Ogata, p.43, citing Playskool catalogue, c.1950. Ethel Kawin was the author of *The Wise Choice of Toys*, 1938. The company was founded by teacher Lucille King in Milwaukee, Wisconsin, in 1928 and moved to Chicago in 1935. Purchased by the Joseph Lumber Company in 1938, it produced a range comparable to Abbatt, and continues as a brand in the ownership of Hasbro since 1984.

146 Atticus, 'What, no Bombs?', *Sunday Times*, 7 May 1950, p.5

147 Amy F. Ogata, op.cit., p.xvi. The phrase is attributed to John H. Lienhard.

148 Jacob Getzells and Philip Jackson, *Creative Intelligence*, (London & New York: John Wiley & Sons, 1962) p.121-22 (note 57). The authors were researchers at the University of Chicago.

149 Atticus (Hunter Davies), 'An Ostrobogulous Year for the toy men', *Sunday Times*, 29 December 1963, p.19; Stevenson quotation from 'A Penny Plain and Twopence Coloured', *Magazine of Art*, vol.VII, 1884, p.232

150 Jack Cross, 'How Action Man derailed a train', *Guardian*, 13 December, 1982.

151 Peter Varley, 'The toymakers of Britain …', *Design* 227, November 1967, p.25

152 Ibid.

153 V&A Museum of Childhood, The papers of (Cyril) Paul Abbatt and (Norah) Marjorie Abbatt, toy manufacturers and educationalists, ca. 1905-1980s. The charitable objectives given officially were 'To promote mental and social education, especially of young children, by means of suitable play activities and other environmental conditions; to improve the technique of early diagnosis, occupational therapy and education in general for children and others suffering from physical, mental and other handicaps; to conduct research and collect scientific material for a comparative study.' The charity was wound up on 6 January 1993. Uk_gov_ccew_portlet_CharitySearchPortlet

154 'Idealists in the Toyshop', *Observer*, 2 December 1962, p.13

155 V&A op.cit.

156 CPA Report, cited in Jude Welton, 1980, p.98

157 Dinah Brook, 'The Pleasant Land of Counterpane', *Observer*, 27 October 1957, p.10. A later comment on the same theme was Moira Keenan, 'Bed and bored', *Sunday Times*, 20 January, 1963, p.36

158 Betty Jerman, 'Children at Play', *Guardian*, 2 January, 1963, p.4

159 Ibid.

160 See Lady Allen of Hurtwood, *Design for Play … the youngest children* (London: Housing Centre Trust and Nursery School Association, 1962) and Jack Lambert, *Adventure Playgrounds* (Harmondsworth, Penguin Books, 1974)

161 Betty Jerman, 'Space to Play', *Observer*, 15 August, 1964, p.5

162 Jude Welton, 1980, p.106

163 *Gutes Spielzeug: Kleines Handbuch für die richtige Wahl*, (issued for the Arbeitsausschuss für Gutes Spielzeug by Otto Maier Verlag, Ravensburg, 1963.

164 Address by Professor John Newson, Degree Ceremony, 10 July, 1981. Cyclostyled pages, Felicity Jaffé archive.

165 Elizabeth Newsom, 'Marjorie Abbatt, a working life in play', *Guardian*, 19 November, 1991, p.37

166 Jack and Elizabeth Hubbard, 'Letter', *Guardian*, 22 November 1991

167 'Interview with Sophie Morgenstern, 12.1.81' (interviewer not identifiable). Felicity Jaffé archive.

168 Eva Brück, 'About Paul and Marjorie Abbatt', manuscript memoir, 10 June 1981. Felicity Jaffé archive. On Eva, see https://de.wikipedia.org/wiki/Eva_Brück.

169 Sophie Morgenstern, op.cit.

170 Abbatt Toys catalogue, 1969-70, p.5

171 'Toys for the Disabled', *The Times*, 1 August, 1968, p.11

172 Betty Jerman, 'Toys for Development', *Guardian*, 9 October 1968, p.9

173 Eva Brück, op.cit.

BIBLIOGRAPHY

Books

Brown, Kenneth D., *The British Toy Business, A History since 1700* (London and Rio Grande: The Hambledon Press, 1996)

Daikin, Leslie. *The World of Toys* (Lambarde Press, 1963

Fraser, Antonia, *A History of Toys* (London: Weidenfeld & Nicolson, 1966)

Gardner, D. M., *Susan Isaacs* (London: Methuen Educational Ltd., 1969)

Graham, Philip, *Susan Isaacs, Freeing the Minds of Young Children* (London: Karnac Books: 2011)

Gutes Spielzeug, Kleines Handbuch für die richtige Wahl (Regensburg: Otto Maier Verlag, 1963)

Isaacs, Susan, *Nursery Years* (London: Routledge & Kegan Paul, 1929)

>*Intellectual Growth in Young* Children (with an Appendix on Children's "Why" Questions by Nathan Isaacs) (London: Routledge and Kegan Paul Ltd., 1930)

>*Behaviour of Young Children* (London: Routledge & Sons, 1930)

Jaffé, Deborah, *The History of Toys from Spinning Tops to Robots* (Stroud: Sutton Publishing, 2006)

Kinchin, Juliet and Aidan O'Connor. *Century of the Child, Growing by Design 1900-2000* (New York: Museum of Modern Art, 2012)

Lowenfeld, Margaret, *Understanding Children's Sandplay: Lowenfeld's World Technique* (Eastbourne: Sussex Academic Press, 2007)

Ogata, Amy F., *Designing the creative child: playthings and places in mid-century America* (Minneapolis: University of Minnesota Press, 2013)

Page, Hilary, *Playtime in the First Five Years* (Croydon: Watson & Crossland, 1939)

Reichardt, Jasia, ed., *Play Orbit* (London and New York: Studio International, 1969)

Steedman, Carolyn, *Childhood, Culture and Class in Britain: Margaret McMillan 1860*-1931 (London: Virago Press, 1990)

Tudor-Hart, Beatrix and Ergy Landau (photographer), *Play and Toys in Nursery Years* (London: Country Life Books, 1938)

Viola, Wilhelm, *Child Art* (Bickley: University of London Press, 1942)

Warburton, Nigel, *Ernö Goldfinger – the life of an architect* (London: Routledge, 2004)

Wells, Herbert George, *Floor Games* (London: Frank Palmer, 1911)

Articles

McKellar, Erin, 'Designing the Child's World: Ernö Goldfinger and the Role of the Architect, 1933-1946', *Journal of Design History*, Volume 33, Issue 1, February 2020, Pages 50–65

Powers, Alan, 'Oliver Hill as an Exhibition Designer', *Thirties Society Journal*, No.7, 1991, pp.28-39

Articles by Paul and Marjorie Abbatt

Abbatt, Marjorie, 'Equipping a Nursery', *Decoration*, January-March, 1935, pp.36-38

Abbatt, Paul, 'The Child's World: Psychology in Toys and Games', *Design for To-day*, vol.1, no.8, December 1933, pp.290-297

Abbatt, Paul, 'The Evolution of Toys', *Design for To-day*, vol.11, no.20, December 1934, pp.442-450

Abbatt, Paul, 'Toys and Play', *Education* (Wellington, NZ), vol.6, no.2, June 1957, pp.30-37

Abbatt, Paul, 'The Place of Toys in a Child's Life: A Commentary on Children, Toys and Play since 1800', in *Number*, vol.3, 1961/2

Obituaries

Paul Abbatt, *The Times*, 16 June, 1971, p.16

Marjorie Abbatt, *Independent*, 13 November 1991 (by Halina Pasierbska)

Marjorie Abbatt, *Guardian*, 19 November 1991 (by Elizabeth Newson)

Journals

Nursery World, The Lady, Toys and Games

Online resources

https://www.vam.ac.uk/moc/british-toy-making-oral-histories/

Oxford Dictionary of National Biography, 'Marjorie Abbatt' by Elizabeth Newson.

Unpublished research

Welton, Jude, *Paul and Marjorie Abbatt: The Story and Ideas behind Abbatt Toys*, University of Nottingham, Child Development Research Unit, 1980

Archive

Victoria and Albert Museum, Museum of Childhood, Bethnal Green, brief listing in https://www.vam.ac.uk/moc/paul-marjorie-abbatt-ltd/

ACKNOWLEDGMENTS

I have long wanted to write about Paul and Marjorie Abbatt, and the opportunity offered by Joe Pearson as a very actively engaged publisher coincided with two other strokes of luck. By chance, Patric Dickinson put me in touch with Marjorie's niece, Felicity Jaffé who shared her happy memories of the couple and their business, where she worked for several years, and lent me a precious box-file of documents, including a copy of the 1980 MA thesis, *Paul and Marjorie Abbatt: The story and ideas behind Abbatt Toys*, written by Jude Welton for the University of Nottingham Child Development Research Unit. This is acknowledged at many points in the book, but attempts to trace the author were sadly unsuccessful. It is an excellent piece of work. The second lucky strike followed an invitation from Margaret Howell and her colleague Richard Craig to propose a theme for one of her annual art and design exhibitions, held at her beautiful shop in Wigmore Street. The Abbatts, whose own shop was only a stone's throw away, seemed an obvious choice of subject, and it has been a pleasure working on it with Jo Barber and Matt Leech on the exhibition, *Abbatt Toys: The Right Toy for the Right Age*.

The text of this book was mainly researched and written during the Covid-19 pandemic of 2020, when it was difficult to carry out archival research in the normal way. Even without this, however, the Abbatt Archive at the V&A Museum of Childhood, Bethnal Green, would probably have been inaccessible owing to the three-year closure for redevelopment. I thought I had seen it all but later discovered I was mistaken and am impatient if anxious to discover in due course what I have missed. I apologise to readers for the omissions that have undoubtedly occurred as a result, but in other ways, it has been possible at least to provide the most complete account published to date of the Abbatts' achievement from other sources.

During the research, I have been helped in various ways by Jane Audas, Eddy Fawdry, Nick and Pippa Goldfinger, Peter Higginson, Richard Hollis, Deborah Jaffé, Chris Mees, David Powell, Janette Ray, Clive Richards, Adrian Shaughnessy, Nick and Sue Smith, and Peter Thorne. I repeat my thanks to Joe Pearson for his patience, encouragement and extraordinary knowledge, and to Laurence Beck for the design of the book. Special thanks, as ever, to Susanna Powers.

PICTURE CREDITS

All items from private collections apart from:

RIBA Photograph Collection: pp.6, 31, 36, 40, 41, 42, 43, 46, 47, 48, 66

Courtesy Harald Eichenberger, Reformpedägogik Unterrichetsentwicklung, p.11

By permission of Rix Pyke, p.14

By permission of Clare Hastings, p.25

Courtesy Pollock's Toy Museum, pp.26-27

Courtesy Adrian Shaughnessy and Ken Garland, p.99

Abbatt cards, prototypes,
designed by Audrey Stephenson